THE SANDS OF KARBALĀʾ

THE EPIC SAGA OF IMĀM ḤUSAYN’S STAND FOR TRUTH

THE SANDS OF KARBALĀʾ

THE EPIC SAGA OF IMĀM ḤUSAYN'S STAND FOR TRUTH

Excerpted from

Tārīkh al-Rusul wa'l-Mulūk -The History of Prophets and Kings

by

Imām Abū Jaʿfar Muḥammad ibn Jarīr ibn Yazīd al-Ṭabarī

Foreword

by

Shaykh Muhammad Hisham Kabbani

INSTITUTE FOR SPIRITUAL & CULTURAL ADVANCEMENT

First Edition July 2025

ISBN: 978-1-938058-88-2

Printed in the United States of America.

Library of Congress Cataloging-in-Publication Data

TBD

Published and Distributed by:
Institute for Spiritual and Cultural Advancement
17195 Silver Parkway, #401
Fenton, MI 48430 USA
Tel: (888) 278-6624
Fax:(810) 815-0518
Email: info@sufilive.com
Web: http://www.sufilive.com

TABLE OF CONTENTS

ABOUT THE AUTHOR 3
FOREWORD 7
Not One Drop of Sayyidinā Ḥusayn's Blood was Shed in Vain! 8
Heavenly Support in Battle 9
Forgiveness When Empowered to Inflict Harm 10
THE EPIC SAGA OF IMĀM ḤUSAYN'S STAND FOR TRUTH 17
The Caliphate of Yazid bin Muawiya 19
Ibn al-Zubayr Withdraws 21
ʿAbd Allāh bin ʿUmar Pledges Allegiance to Yazīd 24
The appointment of ʿAmr ibn Saʿīd as Governor of al-Madīnah 24
ʿAmr ibn al-Zubayr Fights His brother ʿAbd Allāh ibn al-Zubayr....... 25
The Kūfans' Invitation to al-Ḥusayn and the Mission of Muslim ibn ʿAqīl ibn Abī Ṭālib 28
The Killing of Muslim Ibn ʿAqīl 32
Abū Mikhnaf's Account of the Killing of Muslim ibn ʿAqīl............... 33
The People of al-Kūfa Write to al-Ḥusayn 34
Al- Ḥusayn's Letter to the Basrans 40
Another Report of the Killings of Hānī ibn ʿUrwah al-Murādī and Muslim ibn ʿAqīl 45
Muslim Ibn ʿAqīl Responds to the Killing of Hānī ibn ʿUrwa............ 52
The Capture of Muslim Ibn ʿAqīl 57
The Execution of Hānī ibn ʿUrwah 64
Letters between ʿUbayd Allāh ibn Ziyād and Yazīd ibn Muʿāwiyah... 66
Al-Ḥusayn's journey to al-Kūfa 67
The narration of ʿAmmār al-Duhnī from Abū Jaʿfar 75
Zuhayr ibn al-Qayn Joins al-Ḥusayn ibn ʿAlī 83
News of the Killing of Muslim ibn ʿAqīl Reaches al-Ḥusayn.............. 85
Dispersal of the al-Ḥusayn's Iraqi Supporters 87

The Killing of al-Ḥusayn, May Allah be Well Pleased with Him........ 88
ʿUmar ibn Saʿd ibn Abī Waqqāṣ Arrives from al-Kūfa........................ 98
ʿUmar ibn Saʿd Prevents al-Ḥusayn from Reaching Water................ 101
ʿUmar ibn Saʿd's Negotiations with Al-Ḥusayn................................ 102
Shimr ibn Dhī al-Jawshan Urges ʿUmar ibn Saʿd to Fight al-Ḥusayn 105
Al-Ḥusayn Prepares His Men for the Upcoming Battle 109
Al-Ḥusayn Arranges His Troops 112
Al-Ḥusayn's Final Speech 114
Individual Duels Commence... 121
The Companions of al-Ḥusayn Defend His Person 134
The Killing of the Boy al-Qāsim ibn al-Ḥasan ibn ʿAlī...................... 140
Al-Ḥusayn's Final Fight 141
Zaynab Bint Fāṭimah's Rebuke of ʿUbayd Allāh ibn Ziyād.............. 151
The Treatment of ʿAlī ibn al-Ḥusayn.. 151
The Boasting of ʿUbayd Allāh 152
ibn Ziyād 152
The Head of al-Ḥusayn Is Presented to Yazīd ibn Muʿāwiyah 153
Yazīd ibn Muʿāwiyah's Treatment of the Captive Womenfolk of al-Ḥusayn 156
Announcement of the Martyrdom of al-Ḥusayn at al-Madīnah.......... 161
Names of the Companions of al-Ḥusayn Who Were Killed.............. 165

بِسْمِ اللَّهِ الرَّحْمَٰنِ الرَّحِيمِ

قُل لَا أَسْأَلُكُمْ عَلَيْهِ أَجْرًا إِلَّا الْمَوَدَّةَ فِى الْقُرْبَىٰ

Say: I do not ask of you any reward for it but love for my near relatives; (Surat ash-Shūrā 42:23)

إِنَّمَا يُرِيدُ اللَّهُ لِيُذْهِبَ عَنكُمُ الرِّجْسَ أَهْلَ الْبَيْتِ وَيُطَهِّرَكُمْ تَطْهِيرًا

Allah only desires to keep away the uncleanness from you, O people of the House! and to purify you a (thorough) purifying; (Surat al-Ahzāb 33:33)

حَدَّثَنَا ابْنُ نُمَيْرٍ، قَالَ: حَدَّثَنَا عَبْدُ الْمَلِكِ بْنُ أَبِى سُلَيْمَانَ، عَنْ عَطِيَّةَ الْعَوْفِيِّ، عَنْ أَبِى سَعِيدٍ الْخُدْرِيِّ، قَالَ: قَالَ رَسُولُ اللَّهِ ﷺ:
"إِنِّى قَدْ تَرَكْتُ فِيكُمْ مَا إِنْ أَخَذْتُمْ بِهِ لَنْ تَضِلُّوا بَعْدِى: الثَّقَلَيْنِ، أَحَدُهُمَا أَكْبَرُ مِنَ الْآخَرِ، كِتَابُ اللَّهِ حَبْلٌ مَمْدُودٌ مِنَ السَّمَاءِ إِلَى الْأَرْضِ، وَعِتْرَتِى أَهْلُ بَيْتِى، أَلَا وَإِنَّهُمَا لَنْ يَفْتَرِقَا حَتَّى يَرِدَا عَلَىَّ الْحَوْضَ".

The Prophet ﷺ said: I am leaving among you that which if you hold to it, you shall never go astray, one of them greater than the other: Allāh's Book—a rope extended down from the heaven to the earth—and my mantle (*'itra*), the People of my House. These two shall never part ways until they come to me at the Pond. Look well to how you act with them after me.[2]

---

[2] Narrated from Zayd ibn Arqam by al-*Tirmidhī* (*hasan gharīb*) and al-Hākim (3:148)

About the Author

Imām Abū Ja'far Muḥammad ibn Jarīr ibn Yazīd al-Ṭabarī (224–310 AH / 839–923 CE) was one of Islam's greatest historians, exegetes, and jurists.

EARLY LIFE AND EDUCATION

Imām al-Ṭabarī was born in Āmul, the capital of Ṭabaristān (modern-day Māzandarān in northern Iran), in 224 AH / 839 CE. From a young age he showed exceptional aptitude for memorization and scholarship. It is said he memorized the Qur'an by the age of seven and began writing hadith at nine. He left home at around the age of 12 to pursue the Islamic sciences in major centers of learning, a journey that eventually took him across the Islamic world.

Al-Ṭabarī studied under the most renowned scholars of his era in places like Rayy, Baghdad, Kufa, Basra, Wasit, and Egypt. He received knowledge in hadith, fiqh (jurisprudence), Qur'anic *tafsīr* (exegesis), Arabic language, and history. Among his teachers were pupils of Imām Aḥmad ibn Ḥanbal and other leading authorities of the third Islamic century.

SCHOLARLY CONTRIBUTIONS

Imām al-Ṭabarī was a polymath, but his two most enduring works are: *Tafsīr al-Ṭabarī* (*Jāmi' al-Bayān 'an Ta'wīl Āy al-Qur'ān*): A monumental Qur'anic commentary, it combines the rigorous narration of ḥadīth-based *tafsīr* with deep grammatical and theological insight. His *tafsīr* preserves thousands of early interpretations from the Sahabah and Tābi'ūn, making it a primary source for understanding classical Islamic exegesis. He frequently cited authorities such as Ibn 'Abbās, Mujāhid, Qatādah, and others, often giving multiple interpretations and weighing them.

Tārīkh al-Rusul wa'l-Mulūk (*The History of Prophets and Kings*): Also known as *Tārīkh al-Ṭabarī*, this massive work documents the history of the world from the creation of Adam to his own time. It is particularly famous for its detailed account of early Islamic history, including the Prophetic era, the Rightly Guided Caliphs, the Umayyads, and the early 'Abbāsids. Its meticulous chronological narrative and use of *isnād* (chains of transmission) distinguish it from other historical works.

THEOLOGICAL AND JURISTIC VIEWS

Al-Ṭabarī initially studied various legal schools before forming his own independent *madhhab*, which emphasized direct engagement with the Qur'an and Sunnah and rational interpretation within traditional boundaries. His school, though respected, did not gain lasting institutional support and eventually faded. His legal writings, such as *Ikhtilāf al-Fuqahā'* and *Tahdhīb al-Āthār*, show both his juristic acumen and dedication to reconciling hadith evidence.

He was a Sunni Muslim, associated with Ashʿarī theological tendencies in some later evaluations, though in his own time he adhered closely to the traditionalist framework without excessive rationalism. His *tafsīr* often reflects a Salafī-style restraint in speculative theology, while still engaging with *kalām* (theological discourse) when necessary.

OPPOSITION AND LEGACY

Despite his towering scholarship, al-Ṭabarī faced opposition, particularly from some followers of the Ḥanbalī school in Baghdad, who at times harassed him due to theological or juristic differences. He was even prevented from teaching publicly at certain points. Nevertheless, his reputation remained secure among scholars.

He passed away in Baghdad in 310 AH / 923 CE, reportedly on the evening of 27 Shawwāl. He was buried at his home during a period of tension that prevented a public funeral, though later a more prominent burial site was established.

INFLUENCE AND RECOGNITION

Al-Ṭabarī's works remain foundational across disciplines:

Tafsīr al-Ṭabarī is cited by virtually all major Sunni exegetes, including Ibn Kathīr, al-Qurṭubī, and al-Suyūṭī.

Tārīkh al-Ṭabarī is a primary source for the earliest period of Islam and was later abridged and translated into Persian under the patronage of the Samanid court.

His precision in transmission, clarity of style, and objectivity in presenting multiple viewpoints have made him a model of classical Islamic historiography and scriptural interpretation.

Modern scholars, both Muslim and non-Muslim, continue to engage deeply with his legacy, viewing him as one of the most reliable and systematic voices in the early centuries of Islam.

May Allah reward Imām Al-Ṭabarī with an immense reward for the service he has done the Ummah of Prophet Muhammad ﷺ.

FOREWORD

The Shame of the Muslims Is that They Harmed the Grandson of Their Prophet ﷺ

Aʿūdhu billāhi min ash-Shayṭāni 'r-rajīm.
Bismi-llāhi 'r-Raḥmāni 'r-Raḥīm.

As-salāmu ʿalaykum wa raḥmatullāhi wa barakātuh.

Al-ḥamdu li-llāhi Rabbi 'l-ʿĀlamīn, wa 'ṣ-ṣalātu wa 's-salāmu ʿalā ashrafi 'l-mursalīn, Sayyidinā wa Mawlānā Muḥammadin wa ʿalā ālihi wa ṣaḥbihi wa sallim. Al-ḥamdu li-llāhi 'lladhī hadānā li-'l-Islām wa mā kunnā linahtadī law lā an hadānā-llāh.

We are in difficult days; days that we think are overwhelming and we think, "Oh! People are so cruel today." Is that not so? There is so much killing going on, about which Prophet ﷺ said:

يَكْثُرُ الْهَرْجُ وَالْمَرْجُ

Yakthuru 'l-harju wa-'l-marju, and they asked, "What is *harj* and *marj*", and he said "killing, killing, killing!" So today everyone is aware of the evilness of the killing that is taking place everywhere. We know that people today kill to attain an objective: seeking to sit on a chair that is not meant for them. That chair they so eagerly seek will one day belong to someone else. They are fighting for this all around the world, and the cruelty of some people today in killing innocents is broadcast constantly across the Internet and on TV.

Today an important person has a lot of security to protect him. And if something happens to him the whole world becomes worried. So what do you think about an immense event that took place in history? Can you imagine that the child of an important person could be killed? At least for the sake of his father—who is the best in the community or the best in the world—everyone would try to secure the safety of that child. They would secure him with hundreds of people around him. Are we not ashamed as Muslims to do such things? We are ashamed, and what makes us more ashamed is that we are Muslims and harmed other Muslims!

If a Muslim harms a Muslim, all Muslims stand up. Also if a Muslim harms a non-Muslim, everyone stands up against that action, because we are *Ummatan wasaṭan*, the Community of the middle way and we don't practice violence. I can imagine that for a certain reason someone will kill another and for that they put him in jail. But I cannot imagine harming The Most Perfect Human Being ﷺ Allah created among all Heavens and Earth, where all Creation is adorned with his beautiful Light, about which Allah said in Holy Qur'an:

وَاعْلَمُوا أَنَّ فِيكُمْ رَسُولَ اللَّهِ

And know Allah's Messenger is in you. (Sūrat al-Ḥujurāt, 49:7)

Not One Drop of Sayyidinā Ḥusayn's Blood was Shed in Vain!

His Light adorns all humanity, and some irresponsible, jealous, envious ones took revenge from his grandson. Where is *adab*? Today we are suffering here and there, that they killed certain people for certain reasons. Okay, we might understand, but they brought army of 10,000 to kill Sayyidinā Ḥusayn ؓ, the grandson of Sayyidinā Muhammad ﷺ, along with his entire family, wives, and children in cold blood on the 10th Muharram, and that is something which we are remembering in a few days, *inshā-Allah.*

Sayyidinā Ḥusayn ؓ came with 72 people of his own family for what? He came to sacrifice himself for the benefit of the Ummah of Muhammad ﷺ! People told him, "Don't go there," but he said, "I received a lot of letters requesting me to come to Iraq and they will support me." However, they supported the one who opposed him! What, when you gave your promise to support him!

He came in full innocence to see them because he had given them his promised, and he fulfils his promises. They called him to Kufa and to Baghdad, but then what happened? Ḥusayn, the Lion of Allah, the one who, if he says, "*Yā Allah*!" then Allah says, "*Yā ʿabdī* !" and if he says, "*Yā Rasūlullāh, yā Jiddī*!" his grandfather ﷺ will say, "What do you need, my grandson?" The one who with the movement of one arm can eliminate all the people on his right side and with the other arm eliminate all the people on his left side! All that was available to him, but he didn't do that. Why? Because he wants the Ummah to understand that cruelty is not allowed in our religion.

He said to those who petitioned him, "I am coming to you with an open heart." He came towards Iraq to meet with the people, and they responded with *hasad*, envy and jealousy. For what? For the chair! They said, "No, we don't want you; rather we will fight you!" Then when they met for negotiation, Sayyidinā al-Ḥusayn ؓ said, "I will go back, I will go to Damascus, let me go with my family." But they did not accept because they were preparing for that massacre and bloodshed.

Heavenly Support in Battle

Every drop his enemies shed of Sayyidinā al-Ḥusayn's ؓ blood is cursing them, and every drop of his blood was praising Sayyidinā al-Ḥusayn ؓ! If he had wanted, with one arm he could have wiped out the ones on his right side with one motion, just as at the Battle of Badr. There, Allah supported the believers with a thousand angels carrying heavenly swords which, when they moved their swords, all the enemies fell down dead with a black mark on their necks! Just as when Sayyidinā al-Mahdi ؓ comes, he will fight not with a sword nor any weapons but when he calls out "Allahu Akbar!" all the weapons of mass destruction will disintegrate, because justice will have appeared. It will be as if all these weapons of the *dunya* no longer exist with the immense demonstration of Allah's Heavenly Power causing the Earth to absorb these weapons and they will disappear!

With his whip, not even the sword, Sayyidinā al-Mahdi ؓ will whip right or left and reach anyone who opposes peace and harmony, and who opposes what Allah has commanded in order for peace to reign on Earth. Those who oppose it will be taken away and only good people will remain. Thus, when he says *"Allahu Akbar,"* Mahdi ؓ is not going to fight everyone with a sword, no! Grandshaykh ʿAbdAllah al-Fa'iz ad-Daghestani ق said that by the simple motion of one arm, all those on the right will fall down with a black Heavenly Sign on their necks (as if struck by a weapon).

Today, Allah is showing us what the Prophet ﷺ said about this in a hadith, when the Prophet ﷺ was fighting and defeating the unbelievers at the Battle of Badr, where they numbered over 1000 and the Companions numbered only 313, showing them His Greatness. Today Hollywood shows you see people fighting with swords made of light. That is not something that the producers imagined, rather it was thrown into their minds and hearts by the spiritual controllers of this world. Those Hollywood swords are like plastic ones compared to the authentic ones that will be given in the time of Sayyidinā al-Mahdi ؑ!

Forgiveness When Empowered to Inflict Harm

The blood of Sayyidinā al-Ḥusayn ؑ was not shed in vain! Everyone who took part in that battle is going to be judged. Everyone of Ummat an-Nabi ﷺ is definitely going to Paradise, but those who harmed Sayyidinā al-Ḥusayn ؑ are going to be judged. What did Sayyidinā al-Ḥusayn ؑ say to them when they refused to give his children water? What happened when they came to kill him?

He said, "O Earth and O Heavens! You are not going to see anyone like me again." Heaven and Earth wept for him and the sky wept for him, for after this no one on Earth saw the children of Sayyidinā al-Ḥusayn ؑ nor the grandchildren of Sayyidinā al-Ḥusayn. He said this to the head of the army who did not want to fight him, but then the one who sought to instigate the fight, Shimr, threw the first spear and the battle began.

Sayyidinā al-Ḥusayn ؑ possessed *al-ʿafwu ʿinda al-maqdirah*, the ability to forgive despite being in a position to take revenge. "The true forgiveness is in that station of being in power. My grandfather is Sayyidinā Muhammad ﷺ, the Best of Humanity. How are you going to stand in his presence on Judgment Day and you are killing his grandson? What are you going to say about killing his two grandsons?" for Sayyidinā al-Hasan ؑ while not killed at Karbala, was, nevertheless, killed. "What answer do you have? You have no answer, but you know my grandfather, Allah gave me the power:

فَمَن يَعْمَلْ مِثْقَالَ ذَرَّةٍ خَيْرًا يَرَهُ وَمَن يَعْمَلْ مِثْقَالَ ذَرَّةٍ شَرًّا يَرَ

Whosoever has done an atom’s weight of good shall see it, and whosoever has done an atom’s weight of evil shall see it. (Sūrat az-Zalzalah, 99:7-8)

On that day, those who are judged of the good go to Paradise and the rest go to Hellfire, and everyone is in need of the *shafa ʿah* of Rasūlullāh ﷺ! So what are you (I.e. all 10,000 involved in the killing of Sayyidinā al-Ḥusayn) going to say to him? He has the power to throw you in Hellfire by Allah’s Order! Do you think that he will recompense you or punish you? But he ﷺ is not like you; therefore, he will intercede for you. Although he can have you thrown in Hellfire, he will save you on Judgment Day. That is the one whose grandson you seek to kill!”

They killed Sayyidinā al-Ḥusayn ‎رضي الله عنه, beheaded him completely and cut him into pieces, then they took his head and presented it as a gift to the one whose name we hate to mention, who was running the government at that time. It is said that Heavens were weeping with drops of yellow rain, and all kinds of difficulties came upon them after they killed Sayyidinā al-Ḥusayn ‎رضي الله عنه and his family. What did they benefit from that? Nothing!

As Awliyā’ullāh say, “Sayyidinā al-Ḥusayn ‎رضي الله عنه sacrificed himself for the Ummah of the Prophet ﷺ!” Every drop of his blood that was shed was crying out: “Muhammad, Muhammad, Muhammad!” His love for his grandfather ﷺ cannot be explained and his grandfather’s love for him cannot be explained! When they cut off his head, which they say is in different places--either in Karbala or Egypt and was previously in Sham--that head was raised up by angels to the highest level of *Barzakh*, that Heavenly abode between *dunya* and *Akhirah*, and it was replaced by with a replica.

O Muslims! Every Muslim must observe the Day of ʿĀshūrā’ because it is *adab* with Rasūlullāh ﷺ, who said:

أدبنى ربى فأحسن تأديبى

My Lord perfected my good manners and conduct. (Ibn ʿAsākir)

Although he ﷺ is already of good character, when we relate "Allah perfected my character," we must ask: does the Prophet ﷺ have imperfect character? No! So what does it really mean? It means "Allah dressed me from the Light and Manifestation of His Beautiful Names and Attributes," which is to say that Allah ﷻ made him 'lordly':

يَا عَبْدِي أَطِعْنِي أَجْعَلْكَ رَبَّانِيًّا تَقُولُ لِشَيْءٍ كُنْ فَيَكُونُ

O My servant! Obey Me and I will make you lordly; (if) you say to a thing "Be!" it will be (come into existence).

This means, "O My servant! Obey me and I will make you lordly; belong to Me, then when you say to something 'Be!' it will be." Prophet Muhammad ﷺ is the only one with perfect and complete submission to Allah ﷻ. His Ṣaḥābah, Companions, the Awliyā', Saints of Allah, the Ṣiddīqūn, the Testifiers to Truth, the Shuhadā', Martyrs, the Caliphs, the sincere and pious servants of this Ummah, all have been dressed by Allah with perfection, but not in a manner that the Prophet ﷺ has been. Allah gave them perfection, but not like that of the Prophet ﷺ for all of them still need to ascend higher and higher. Therefore, for Ahlu 's-Sunnah wa 'l-Jamā'ah, at the very least it is *adab* to remember that day. If those who hold other beliefs don't want to observe that day we understand, but we, as Ahlu 's-Sunnah wa 'l-Jamā'ah must observe that day and on that day we must also relate the story of Sayyidinā al-Ḥusayn ؑ to our children because it teaches us how to be perfect. And we fast on that day as the Prophet ﷺ has mentioned two hadiths on the importance of that fast.

فِي رِوَايَةٍ لِمُسْلِمٍ عَنِ ابْنِ عَبَّاسٍ رَضِيَ ٱللَّهُ عَنْهُمَا، أَنَّ رَسُولَ ٱللَّهِ ﷺ قَدِمَ ٱلْمَدِينَةَ، فَوَجَدَ ٱلْيَهُودَ صِيَامًا يَوْمَ عَاشُورَاءَ، فَقَالَ لَهُمْ رَسُولُ ٱللَّهِ ﷺ: "مَا هَذَا ٱلْيَوْمُ ٱلَّذِي تَصُومُونَهُ؟"

فَقَالُوا: "هَذَا يَوْمٌ عَظِيمٌ، أَنْجَى ٱللَّهُ فِيهِ مُوسَىٰ وَقَوْمَهُ، وَغَرَّقَ فِرْعَوْنَ وَقَوْمَهُ، فَصَامَهُ مُوسَىٰ شُكْرًا، فَنَحْنُ نَصُومُهُ".

فَقَالَ رَسُولُ ٱللَّهِ ﷺ: "فَنَحْنُ أَحَقُّ وَأَوْلَىٰ بِمُوسَىٰ مِنْكُمْ." فَصَامَهُ رَسُولُ ٱللَّهِ ﷺ، وَأَمَرَ بِصِيَامِهِ.

Ibn `Abbas ؓ reported that the Prophet ﷺ arrived in Madina and found the Jews observing fast on the day of ʿĀshūrā’. The Prophet ﷺ said to them: “What is the (significance) of this day that you observe fast on it?” They said: “It is the day of great (significance) when Allah delivered Moses and his people, and drowned the Pharaoh and his people, and Moses observed fast out of gratitude and we also observe it.” Upon this the Messenger of Allah ﷺ said: “We have more right, and we have a closer connection with Moses than you have.” So Allah’s Messenger ﷺ observed fast (on the day of ʿĀshūrā’), and gave orders that it should be observed. (Muslim)

Also the day of ʿĀshūrā’ was fasted in the time before the fast Ramadan became obligatory. Originally it was an obligatory fast, and they then stopped fasting on ʿĀshūrā’ after the fast of Ramadan was made obligatory. So we fast not only in honor of Sayyidinā Musa ؑ and the Children of Israel being saved, but also in honor of Sayyidinā al-Ḥusayn ؑ. Also on that day, Allah forgave Sayyidinā Adam ؑ, and on that day Allah saved Sayyidinā Nuh ؑ from the flood, and saved Sayyidinā Ibrahim ؑ from the fire of Nimrood, and on that day Allah saved Sayyidinā Musa ؑ from Pharaoh, on that day Allah saved Sayyidinā `Isa ؑ by raising him up, and on that day Allah dressed the Prophet ﷺ completely with many adornments and divine manifestations. So we, as Ahlu ‘s-Sunnah wa ‘l-Jamāʿah, must recall the story of Sayyidinā Ḥusayn ؑ, for that is not only a Shi`a concept, but it is an Ahlu ‘s-Sunnah wa ‘l-Jamāʿah concept--to observe and learn from him, and how he took 70 people with him and they were massacred and cut into pieces. That was in order for the whole Ummah to be saved. Unlike what is happening in Middle Eastern countries now, where killing is taking place everywhere with nor rhyme or reason only killing to take over the chair.

No one can bring back peace to Earth except by Allah’s order and the Prophet’s ﷺ order, as he ﷺ mentioned in a hadith of the Last Days, that Mahdi will come with peace and justice and balance.

الْمَهْدِيُّ مِنِّي أَجْلَى الْجَبْهَةِ أَقْنَى الأَنْفِ يَمْلأُ الأَرْضَ قِسْطًا وَعَدْلاً كَمَا مُلِئَتْ جَوْرًا وَظُلْمًا يَمْلِكُ سَبْعَ سِنِينَ

The Mahdi will be of my descendants and will have a broad forehead, a prominent nose. He will fill the Earth will equity and justice as it was filled with oppression and tyranny, and he will rule for seven years. (Abū Dāwūd)

ٱلْمَهْدِيُّ مِنِّي، أَجْلَى ٱلْجَبْهَةِ، أَقْنَى ٱلأَنْفِ، يَمْلَأُ ٱلأَرْضَ قِسْطًا وَعَدْلاً كَمَا مُلِئَتْ جَوْرًا وَظُلْمًا، يَمْلِكُ سَبْعَ سِنِينَ.

Justice here means "Justice between Muslim and non-Muslim" and between everyone, not war, using machine guns, artillery and missiles and beheading people as that is not Islam. It is not mentioned in any hadith that he will take over the countries with missiles and cannons and fire, no; when any hadith is mentioned about Mahdi ﷺ it mentions peace. When he says "*Allahu Akbar*" that means peace, for Allah is Greater than everything! By this word all the weapons will melt. May Allah ﷻ teach us good manners!

During one of his forty-day seclusions Grandshaykh ق said that:

وصيّةُ اللهِ للحبيبِ: لا تَنسَ الأدبَ

Waṣiyyatullāh li 'l-ḥabīb lā tansā al-adab, the advice of Allah to the Prophet ﷺ is, "Don't forget *adab*." That is why the Prophet ﷺ sought and seeks to teach the Ummah good *adab* and that advice is ongoing for the Ummah, as the Prophet's ﷺ adab was already perfected by his Lord! What is *adab*?

أَوْصَى النَّبِيُّ ﷺ أَبَا هُرَيْرَةَ بِوَصِيَّةٍ عَظِيمَةٍ، فَقَالَ: "يَا أَبَا هُرَيْرَةَ! عَلَيْكَ بِحُسْنِ الْخُلُقِ".
قَالَ أَبُو هُرَيْرَةَ رَضِىَ اللهُ عَنْهُ: "وَمَا حُسْنُ الْخُلُقِ يَا رَسُولَ اللهِ؟"
قَالَ ﷺ: "تَصِلُ مَنْ قَطَعَكَ، وَتَعْفُو عَمَّنْ ظَلَمَكَ، وَتُعْطِى مَنْ حَرَمَكَ".

The Prophet ﷺ advised Abu Hurayrah with a tremendous advice: "O Abaa Hurayrah! You must have the best of manners." Abu Hurayrah asked, "What are the best of manners, O Rasūlullāh ﷺ?" He ﷺ said, "Connect with the one who cut you off; forgive the one who oppressed you and give to the one who prevented you from reaching your desires." (Al-Bayhaqi)

It is not good manners to cut off innocent people's heads and that mistaken action falls not only on the executioners, but that mistake falls on every leader in this world that allow this misery to continue like that, as the Prophet ﷺ mentioned in hadith, where his hadith predicted all issues of yesterday and today, and one of them is:

أَبْشِرُوا بِالْمَهْدِيِّ، رَجُلٌ مِنْ قُرَيْشٍ مِنْ عِتْرَتِى، يَخْرُجُ فِى اخْتِلَافٍ مِنَ النَّاسِ وَزَلَازِلَ،
فَيَمْلَأُ الْأَرْضَ قِسْطًا وَعَدْلًا كَمَا مُلِئَتْ جَوْرًا وَظُلْمًا.

Good tidings of al-Mahdi, a man from the Quraysh from my descendants, who will appear during a (time of) great dissension between the people and earthquakes, and he will fill the Earth with justice and fairness as much as it had been filled with harm and oppression. (al-Ḥākim)

May Allah ﷻ show us those days. And now we will read a special Surat al-Fatihah for Sayyidinā al-Ḥusayn ؓ and those who died with him and for all the Ahlu 'l-Bayt ؓm the Family of the Prophet ﷺ. We recite al-Fatiha for the honor of the Beloved.

Mawlana Shaykh Muhammad Hisham Kabbani
'Āshūrā', 1 November 2014
Fenton Michigan, USA

THE SANDS OF KARBALĀ’

THE EPIC SAGA OF IMĀM ḤUSAYN’S STAND FOR TRUTH

The Caliphate of Yazid bin Muawiya

In this year 60 AH/680 CE, Yazīd bin Mu'āwiya ﷺ was pledged allegiance as caliph after the death of his father, on the 15th of Rajab (April 22, 680) according to some, and according to others, when eight days remained from it - as we mentioned before about the death of his father Mu'āwiya. He confirmed 'Ubayd Allāh bin Ziyād as governor over Basra, and al-Nu'mān bin Bashīr over Kufa.

Hishām bin Muḥammad said, on the authority of Abū Mikhnaf, Yazīd took over in the new moon of Rajab in the year 60, and the governor of al-Madīna at that time was al-Walīd bin 'Utba bin Abī Sufyān, the governor of Kufa was al-Nu'mān bin Bashīr al-Anṣārī ﷺ, the governor of Basra was 'Ubayd Allāh bin Ziyād, and the governor of Mecca was 'Amr bin Sa'īd bin al-'Āṣ. Yazīd had no other ambition when he took over but to secure the allegiance of those who refused to pledge allegiance when Mu'āwiya had called people to pledge allegiance to Yazīd, and that he was his successor after him, and Yazīd sought to finish the matter. So he wrote to al-Walīd:

> In the name of Allah, the Most Gracious, the Most Merciful, from Yazīd, the Commander of the Faithful, to al-Walīd bin 'Utba. To proceed, Mu'āwiya was a servant of Allah, whom Allah honored and made his successor, and granted him, and empowered him. He lived by measure and died as fated. May Allah have mercy on him, for he lived praiseworthy and died righteous and pious. Peace be upon you.

And he wrote to him on a piece of paper the size of a rat's ear:

> To proceed, seize Ḥusayn, 'Abd Allāh bin 'Umar and 'Abd Allāh bin al-Zubayr to take pledge allegiance showing no leniency until they give the oath. Peace be with you.

When the news of Mu'āwiya's death reached al-Walīd, he was shocked and it weighed heavily upon him. He sent for Marwān bin al-Ḥakam. When al-Walīd had first arrived in al-Madīna, Marwān only visited him with reluctance. When al-Walīd saw that from him, he insulted him before his courtiers. Marwān heard about it, so he stayed away from him and cut him off. It remained so until the news of Mu'āwiya's death reached al-Walīd. When the death of Mu'āwiya hung heavy upon al-Walīd and what he had been ordered to do regarding taking the pledge of allegiance from these people, he was alarmed and called for Marwān. When he read Yazīd's letter to him, he said "*Inna lillahi wa inna ilayhi raji'un, We belong to God and to Him we shall return*" and prayed for mercy upon him.

Al-Walīd consulted him saying: "What do you think we should do?" He said: "I think you should immediately send for these people and call them to pledge allegiance and enter obedience. If they do, accept it from them and spare them. If they refuse, bring them forward and strike their necks before they learn about Mu'āwiya's death. If they know about Mu'āwiya's death, each of them will rise from a different side, show opposition and rebellion, and call men to himself. But in the case of Ibn 'Umar, I don't think he would consider fighting, nor does he like to be in charge of people, unless the matter is handed to him willingly."

So, he sent 'Abd Allāh bin 'Amr bin 'Uthmān - who was a young boy at that time - to them to call the two of them, al-Ḥusayn ؓ and 'Abd Allāh bin al-Zubayr ؓ. He found them in the mosque sitting, and he came to them at a time when al-Walīd did not usually sit with the people, so they would not go to him at such a time. He said: "Answer, the governor's call to you both." They said to him: "Go back, we will come to him now." Then one of them turned to the other and 'Abd Allāh bin al-Zubayr said to Ḥusayn: "What do you think he sent for us at this hour when he does not usually sit with his court?" Ḥusayn said: "I suspect their tyrant has perished, so he sent for us to take the pledge of allegiance before the news spreads among the people." Ibn al-Zubayr said: "And I don't believe it can be anything else." Ibn al-Zubayr said: "What do you want to do?" Ḥusayn said: "I will gather my young men now, then I will go to him. When I reach the door, I will keep them there, then I will enter upon him."

Ibn al-Zubayr said: "I fear for you if you enter." Ḥusayn said: "I will not go in to him unless I am in a position to refuse." So he stood up, gathered his supporters and family members and then walked until he reached the door of al-Walīd saying to his companions: "I am entering. If I call you or you hear his voice raised, then storm in all together. Otherwise, do not leave until I come out to you."

He entered and greeted him the governor, and Marwān was sitting with him. Ḥusayn said, as if he did not suspect the death of Mu'āwiya had occurred:

"Reconciliation is better than separation. May Allah mend your relationship!" They did not respond to him in this matter, and he came and sat down. Al-Walīd read the letter to him and informed him of Muʿāwiya's death and invited him to pledge allegiance. Al-Ḥusayn said: "*Indeed, we belong to Allah and to Him we shall return*! May Allah have mercy on Muʿāwiya and magnify your reward! As for what you asked me about the pledge of allegiance, someone like me does not give his pledge secretly. And I do not see you being satisfied with it being done by me secretly without showing it publicly to the people." He said: "Yes." He said: "So when you go out to the people and invite them to pledge allegiance, invite us with the people so that it is one matter."

Al-Walīd, who loved peace, said to him: "Leave in the name of Allah until you come to us with the group of people." Marwān said to him: "By Allah, if he leaves you now without pledging allegiance, you will never be able to get the same opportunity from him until many are killed between you and him. Detain the man and do not let him leave until he pledges allegiance or you strike his neck." At that, Ḥusayn jumped up and said: "O son of the blue-eyed woman, will you kill me or would he? By Allah, you lied and sinned." Then he left and passed by his companions, and they went out with him until he reached his house.

Marwān said to al-Walīd: "You disobeyed me. By Allah, you will never be able to get the same opportunity from him again." Al-Walīd said: "Rebuke someone else, O Marwān. You chose for me what would destroy my religion. By Allah, I would not love that I possess whatever the sun rises and sets over of the wealth and kingdom of this world, in return for killing al-Ḥusayn. Glory be to Allah! Should I kill al-Ḥusayn if he says: 'I will not pledge allegiance!' By Allah, I do not think a person who is held accountable for the blood of al-Ḥusayn will have a light scale with Allah on the Day of Judgment." Marwān said to him: "If this is your opinion, then you have done well in what you did." He said this to him without commending his opinion.

Ibn al-Zubayr Withdraws

As for Ibn al-Zubayr, he said: "I will come to you now." Then he went to his house and hid there. Al-Walīd sent to him and found him gathered with his companions, on guard. He pressured him with many messengers one man following another. As for Ḥusayn, he said: "Wait until you see and we see, and you observe and we observe." As for Ibn al-Zubayr, he said: "Do not rush me, for I will come to you. Give me time." They harassed them throughout that evening and the beginning of their night but they were easier on al-Ḥusayn. Al-Walīd sent his supporters to Ibn al-Zubayr and they insulted him and shouted at him: "O son of the diviner, by Allah, you will come to the governor or he will kill you." He remained like that all day and into the beginning of his night, saying: "I will come now." When they urged him, he said: "By Allah, I have become suspicious due to the many messages and the succession of these men. Do not rush me until I send to the governor someone who will bring me his opinion and command." He sent to him his brother Jaʿfar ibn al-Zubayr, who said: "May Allah have mercy on you! Stop bothering ʿAbd Allāh, for you have frightened and alarmed him with your many messengers. He will come to you tomorrow, God willing. Order your messengers to leave us." Al-Walīd sent to them, and they left. Ibn al-Zubayr set out under cover of night and took the road to al-Furʿ, along with his brother Jaʿfar.

There was no third person with them, and they avoided the main road for fear of being pursued, and they headed towards Mecca. When morning came, al-Walīd sent for him and found that he had left. Marwān said: "By Allah, if he missed Mecca, then send men after him." He sent a horseman from the Mawālī of Banū Umayya along with eighty riders. They searched for him but could not find him, so they returned. They were preoccupied with searching for ʿAbd Allāh that day until evening. Then he sent men to Ḥusayn in the evening and said: "Wait until morning, then you will see and we will see." They left him alone that night and did not press him. Ḥusayn left during the night, which was Sunday night, with two days remaining in Rajab of the year 60 AH.

Ibn al-Zubayr had left the night before, on Saturday night, taking the road to al-Furʿ. While ʿAbd Allāh ibn al-Zubayr was walking with his brother Jaʿfar, Jaʿfar recited the words of Ṣabra al-Ḥanẓalī:

> And all the sons of mother
> will find one night
> that none of their descendants
> will remain except one.

ʿAbd Allāh said: "Glory be to Allah, what did you mean by what I hear, O my brother!" He said: "By Allah, O my brother, I did not mean anything that you dislike." He said: "By Allah, I dislike even more that it came from your tongue unintentionally." It was as if he took it as an omen.

As for al-Ḥusayn, he left with his sons, brothers, nephews, and most of his family, except for Muḥammad ibn al-Ḥanafiyya. He said to him: "O my brother, you are the most beloved of people to me and the dearest to me. I do not withhold advice from anyone more deserving of it than you. Keep yourself away from Yazīd ibn Muʿāwiya and the cities as much as you can. Then send your messengers to the people and invite them to yourself. If they pledge allegiance to you, praise Allah for that. If the people agree on someone else, it will not diminish your religion, intellect, dignity, or virtue. I fear that you will enter one of these cities and a group of people will come to you. They will differ among themselves, some with you and others against you. They will fight, and you will be the first to be attacked. Then you will be the best of this nation in soul and father, but the most squandered in blood and the most humiliated in family."

Al-Ḥusayn said to him: "I am going, O my brother." He said: "Stay in Mecca. If you feel safe there, then that is good. If not, then head to the deserts and the mountain peaks. Move from place to place until you see what becomes of the people's affairs. You will then know the right opinion. You will be most correct in opinion and most decisive in action when you face matters head-on. Matters will never be more confusing to you than when you look back on them." Al-Ḥusayn said: "O my brother, you have advised and shown concern. I hope your opinion is sound and successful."

Abū Mikhnaf related: ʿAbd al-Malik bin Nawfal bin Masāḥiq narrated to me, from Abū Saʿd al-Maqburī, who said: "I saw al-Ḥusayn entering the mosque of al-Madīna, and he was walking while leaning on two men, relying on this one once and on that one once, and he was reciting the words of Ibn Mufarrigh:

> I did not frighten the cattle at dawn
> as a raider, nor did I call Yazīd
> On the day I gave up some of my awe
> and death was watching me to turn away.

He said: 'I said to myself: By Allah, he did not recite these two verses except for something he intends.' He said: 'He did not stay more than two days until I heard that he had traveled to Mecca.'"

'Abd Allāh bin 'Umar Pledges Allegiance to Yazīd

Then al-Walīd sent to 'Abd Allāh bin 'Umar ؓ and said: "Pledge allegiance to Yazīd." He said: "If the people pledge allegiance, I will pledge allegiance." A man said: "What prevents you from pledging allegiance? You only want the people to differ, fight, and perish. When they are exhausted, they will say: 'Turn to 'Abd Allāh bin 'Umar, there is no one left but him, pledge allegiance to him!'" 'Abd Allāh said: "I do not want them to fight, differ, or perish, but if the people pledge their allegiance and there is no one left but me, I will pledge my allegiance." He said: "So they left him alone and did not fear him."

Ibn al-Zubayr ؓ went on until he reached Mecca, and 'Amr bin Sa'īd was governor there. When he entered Mecca, he said: "I am only seeking refuge." He did not pray with their prayers, nor did he perform the rituals with their rituals. He would stand with his companions aside, then perform the rituals with them alone, and pray with them alone.

When al-Ḥusayn ؓ headed towards Mecca, he said: 'So he left it, fearing, watching. He said: "*My Lord, save me from the wrongdoing people.*" (Sūrat al-Qaṣaṣ 28:21) When he entered Mecca, he said: "*And when he turned his face towards Midian, he said: 'Perhaps my Lord will guide me to the right way.'*" (Sūrat al-Kahf, 18:22)

The appointment of 'Amr ibn Sa'īd as Governor of al-Madīnah

In this year 60, Yazīd dismissed al-Walīd ibn 'Utbah from al-Madīnah in the month of Ramadan, and appointed 'Amr ibn Sa'īd al-Ashdaq over it. Al-Wāqidī claimed that Ibn 'Umar was not in al-Madīnah at arrival of the news of Mu'āwiyah's death and the demand for pledge of allegiance to Yazīd, and that Ibn al-Zubayr and al-Ḥusayn, when they were called to pledge allegiance to Yazīd, refused and left that night to Makkah. They met Ibn 'Abbās and Ibn 'Umar coming from Makkah, and they asked them, "What is behind you?" They said: "The death of Mu'āwiyah and the pledge of allegiance to Yazīd." Ibn ʿUmar said to them: "Fear Allah and do not divide the community of Muslims." As for Ibn ʿUmar, he came and stayed for a few days, waiting until the pledge of allegiance came from the regions. Then he went to al-Walīd ibn ʿUtbah and pledged allegiance to him, and Ibn ʿAbbās also pledged allegiance to him.

ʿAmr ibn al-Zubayr Fights His brother ʿAbd Allāh ibn al-Zubayr

In this year, ʿAmr ibn Saʿīd sent ʿAmr ibn al-Zubayr to fight his brother ʿAbd Allāh ibn al-Zubayr. (Mention of the news about that:) Muḥammad ibn ʿUmar mentioned that ʿAmr ibn Saʿīd ibn al-ʿĀṣ al-Ashdaq came to al-Madīnah in Ramadan of the year sixty, and the people of al-Madīnah entered upon him, and they entered upon a man of great arrogance and eloquence.

Muḥammad ibn ʿUmar said: Hishām ibn Saʿīd narrated to us, from Shaybah ibn Naṣāḥ, he said: Messengers were running between Yazīd ibn Muʿāwiyah and Ibn al-Zubayr regarding the pledge of allegiance, and Yazīd swore that he would not accept it from him until he was brought to him in chains. Al-Ḥārith ibn Khālid al-Makhzūmī was in charge of leading the prayer, but Ibn al-Zubayr prevented him. When he prevented him, Yazīd wrote to ʿAmr ibn Saʿīd to send an army against Ibn al-Zubayr. When ʿAmr ibn Saʿīd came to al-Madīnah, he appointed ʿAmr ibn al-Zubayr as his police chief, knowing the enmity between him and [his brother] ʿAbd Allāh ibn al-Zubayr. He sent for a group of the people of al-Madīnah and whipped them severely. Muḥammad ibn ʿUmar said: Shuraḥbīl ibn Abī ʿAwn narrated to me, from his father, he said: He looked at everyone who was inclined towards Ibn al-Zubayr and had them beaten. Among those he had flogged were al-Mundhir ibn al-Zubayr, his son Muḥammad ibn al-Mundhir, ʿAbd al-Raḥmān ibn al-Aswad ibn ʿAbd Yaghūth, ʿUthmān ibn ʿAbd Allāh ibn Ḥakīm ibn Ḥizām, Khubayb ibn ʿAbd Allāh ibn al-Zubayr, and Muḥammad ibn ʿAmmār ibn Yāsir. He beat them from forty to fifty to sixty lashes.

ʿAbd al-Raḥmān ibn ʿUthmān and ʿAbd al-Raḥmān ibn ʿAmr ibn Sahl fled with some people to Makkah. ʿAmr ibn Saʿīd said to ʿAmr ibn al-Zubayr: "Who is the man we should send to your brother?" He said: "You cannot send anyone against him more harmful to him than myself." He brought out tens of the people of proscription, and many of the clients of the people of al-Madīnah (*mawali*) went out with him. Unays ibn ʿAmr al-Aslamī went out with seven hundred men, and he sent him at the forefront. He camped at al-Jurf. Marwān ibn al-Ḥakam came to ʿAmr ibn Saʿīd and said: "Do not invade Makkah, fear Allah, and do not violate the sanctity of the House. Leave Ibn al-Zubayr, for he has grown old. He is over sixty years old, and he is a stubborn man. By Allah, if you do not kill him, he will die." ʿAmr ibn al-Zubayr said: "By Allah, we will fight him and invade him inside the Kaʿbah regardless of those who are displeased." Marwān said: "By Allah, that would displease me." Unays ibn ʿAmr al-Aslamī marched until he camped at Dhū Ṭuwā, and ʿAmr ibn al-Zubayr marched until he camped at al-Abṭaḥ. ʿAmr ibn al-Zubayr sent to his brother: "Fulfill the allegiance to the caliph and put a silver chain around your neck that cannot be seen, so that people do not strike each other. Fear Allah, for you are in a sacred land." Ibn al-Zubayr said: "Your appointment is at the mosque." Ibn al-Zubayr sent ʿAbd Allāh ibn Ṣafwān al-Jumaḥī to Unays ibn ʿAmr from Dhū Ṭuwā. A group of people who had settled around Makkah had joined ʿAbd Allāh ibn Ṣafwān. They fought Unays ibn ʿAmr, and Unays ibn ʿAmr was defeated in the worst sort of way. Most of ʿAmr's companions dispersed from him and he entered the house of ʿAlqamah. ʿUbaydah ibn al-Zubayr came to him and granted him protection. Then he went to ʿAbd Allāh ibn al-Zubayr and said: "I have granted him safe conduct," and he said: "Do you grant him safe conduct from the rights of the people?! This is not appropriate."

Muḥammad ibn ʿUmar said: I narrated this story to Muḥammad ibn ʿUbayd ibn ʿUmayr, and he said: ʿAmr ibn Dīnār informed me, saying: Yazīd ibn Muʿāwiyah wrote to ʿAmr ibn Saʿīd: "Appoint ʿAmr ibn al-Zubayr over the army, and send him to Ibn al-Zubayr, and send Unays ibn ʿAmr with him." He said: ʿAmr ibn al-Zubayr marched until he settled in his house near al-Ṣafā, and Unays ibn ʿAmr settled at Dhū Ṭuwā. ʿAmr ibn al-Zubayr used to lead the people in prayer, and ʿAbd Allāh ibn al-Zubayr prayed behind him. When he finished, he intertwined his fingers together, and no one from Quraysh remained except that they came to ʿAmr ibn al-Zubayr. ʿAbd Allāh ibn Ṣafwān sat and to ʿAmr said: "Why do I not see ʿAbd Allāh ibn Ṣafwān! By Allah, if I march to him, he will know that the Banū Jumaḥ and those who joined him from others are few." ʿAbd Allāh ibn Ṣafwān heard this statement and it moved him. He said to ʿAbd Allāh ibn al-Zubayr: "I see that you want to spare your brother." ʿAbd Allāh said: "I spare him, O Abū Ṣafwān! By Allah, if I could use the help of ants against him, I would use it." Ibn Ṣafwān said: "I will take care of Unays ibn ʿAmr for you, so take care of your brother for me." Ibn al-Zubayr said: "Yes."

ʿAbd Allāh ibn Ṣafwān marched to Unays ibn ʿAmr while he was at Dhū Ṭuwā, and he met him with a large group of people from Makkah and other supporters. They defeated Unays ibn ʿAmr and those with him, killed their retreating ones, and finished off their wounded ones. Muṣʿab ibn ʿAbd al-Raḥmān marched to ʿAmr, and his companions dispersed from him until he reached ʿAmr ibn al-Zubayr. ʿUbaydah ibn al-Zubayr said to ʿAmr: "Come, I will grant you protection." ʿAbd Allāh ibn al-Zubayr came and said: "I have granted ʿAmr safe conduct, therefore grant him safe conduct for me." He refused to grant him safe conduct, and he beat him as he had beaten those in al-Madīnah, and imprisoned him in the harsh prison.

Al-Wāqidī said: They differed with us in the story of ʿAmr ibn al-Zubayr, and I wrote all of that. Khālid ibn Ilyās narrated to me, from Abū Bakr ibn ʿAbd Allāh ibn Abī al-Jahm, he said: When ʿAmr ibn Saʿīd came to al-Madīnah as governor, he came in Dhū al-Qaʿdah of the year sixty, and he appointed ʿAmr ibn al-Zubayr as his police chief.

He said:

> The Commander of the Faithful has sworn that he will not accept the pledge of allegiance from Ibn al-Zubayr unless he is brought in chains. Let the Commander of the Faithful fulfill his oath, for I will make light chains from paper or gold, and he will wear a cloak over them, and they will not be seen except that their sound will be heard."

He said:

> Take it, truly it is not the right course for the noble
> In it is a statement for a humiliated person
> O ʿĀmir, the people have imposed a course on you
> And you would have no blame among the neighbors

Muḥammad said: Rīyāḥ ibn Muslim narrated to me, from his father, he said: ʿAmr ibn Saʿīd sent to ʿAbd Allāh ibn al-Zubayr, and Abū Shurayḥ said to him: "Do not invade Makkah, for I heard the Messenger of Allah ﷺ say:

'Allah only permitted me to fight in Makkah for an hour of the day, then it returned to its sanctity.'" But ʿAmr refused to listen to his words and said: "We know its sanctity better than you, old man."

So ʿAmr sent an army with ʿAmr and with him Unays ibn ʿAmr al-Aslamī, and Zayd, the servant of Muḥammad ibn ʿAbd Allāh ibn al-Ḥārith ibn Hishām, and they were about two thousand. The people of Makkah fought them, and Unays ibn ʿAmr and al-Muhājir, the servant of al-Qalammas, were killed among many others, and ʿAmr's army was defeated. ʿUbaydah ibn al-Zubayr came and said to his brother ʿAmr: "You are under my protection, and I am your protector." So he took him to ʿAbd Allāh, and he entered upon Ibn al-Zubayr and said: "What is this blood on your face, you wicked one!" ʿAmr said:

> Our wounds bleed not on the heels
> But on our feet is where the blood drips

So he imprisoned him and dishonored ʿUbaydah's offer of protection, and said: "Did I order you to protect this sinner who violates the sanctities of Allah?" Then he exacted retribution from ʿAmr for everyone he had beaten except al-Mundhir and his son, for they refused to seek retribution. ʿAmr died under the lashes.

He said: The prison was named ʿĀrim for a servant who was called Zayd ʿĀrimin which Ibn al-Zubayr imprisoned his brother ʿAmir.

The Kūfans' Invitation to al-Ḥusayn and the Mission of Muslim ibn ʿAqīl ibn Abī Ṭālib

Al-Wāqidī said: ʿAbd Allāh ibn Abī Yaḥyā narrated to us, from his father, he said: Unays ibn ʿAmr had two thousand men with him. In this year, the people of al-Kūfah sent messengers to al-Ḥusayn ﷺ while he was in Makkah, inviting him to come to them. He sent to them his cousin Muslim ibn ʿAqīl ibn Abī Ṭālib (may Allah be pleased with him). (Mention of the news about the correspondence of the people of al-Kūfah with al-Ḥusayn ﷺ to come to them and the matter of Muslim ibn ʿAqīl (may Allah be pleased with him):) Zakariyyā ibn Yaḥyā al-Ḍarīr narrated to me, he said: Aḥmad ibn Janāb al-Muṣiṣī, who was known as Abū al-Walīd, narrated to us, he said: Khālid ibn Yazīd ibn Asad ibn ʿAbd Allāh al-Qasrī narrated to us, he said: ʿAmmār al-Duhnī narrated to us, he said: I said to Abū Jaʿfar: "Tell me about the killing of al-Ḥusayn as if I were present." He said: "Muʿāwiyah died and al-Walīd ibn ʿUtbah ibn Abī Sufyān was governor over al-Madīnah. He sent to al-Ḥusayn ibn ʿAlī to take his pledge of allegiance. Al-Ḥusayn said to him: 'Give me time and be lenient.' So he delayed him, and al-Ḥusayn set out for Makkah. The people of al-Kūfah and their messengers came to him, saying: 'We have confined ourselves only to you, and we do not attend the Friday prayer with the governor. Come to us.' Al-Nuʿmān ibn Bashīr al-Anṣārī was governor over al-Kūfah. Al-Ḥusayn sent for Muslim ibn ʿAqīl ibn Abī Ṭālib, his cousin, and said to him: 'Go to al-Kūfah and see what they have written to me. If it is true, we will go to them.' Muslim went until he came to al-Madīnah, and he took two guides from there. They traveled through the desert, and they were afflicted by thirst. One of the guides died, and Muslim wrote to al-Ḥusayn asking to be excused. Al-Ḥusayn wrote to him: 'Proceed to al-Kūfah.'"

He set out until he arrived there, and he stayed with a man from its people called Ibn ʿAwsajah. He said: When the people of al-Kūfah heard of his arrival, they flocked to him and pledged allegiance to him. Twelve thousand of them pledged allegiance to him. He said: A man who favored Yazīd ibn Muʿāwiyah went to al-Nuʿmān ibn Bashīr and said to him: "You are weak or pretending to be weak, the country has become corrupt!" Al-Nuʿmān said to him: "To be weak while obeying Allah is more beloved to me than to be strong while disobeying Allah, and I would not expose a cover that Allah has concealed." Al-Nuʿmān wrote to Yazīd about the situation.

Yazīd called a servant of his named Sarjūn, who used to consult him, and informed him of the news. He said to him: "Would you have accepted from Muʿāwiyah if he were alive?" He said: "Yes." He said: "Then accept from me, for there is no one for al-Kūfah except ʿUbayd Allāh ibn Ziyād. Appoint him over it."

Yazīd was angry with ʿUbayd Allāh ibn Ziyād and intended to remove him from al-Baṣrah. [Following Sarjun's advice] he wrote to him expressing his satisfaction and that he had appointed him over al-Kūfah along with al-Baṣrah, and wrote to him to seek out Muslim ibn ʿAqīl and kill him if he found him.

ʿUbayd Allāh came with the nobles of the people of al-Baṣrah until he arrived at al-Kūfah, with his face veiled. He did not pass by any gathering of people and greet them except that they said: "Peace be upon you, O son of the daughter of the Messenger of Allah," thinking that he was al-Ḥusayn ibn ʿAlī. He descended at the palace, called a servant of his, gave him three thousand dirhams, and said to him: "Go and ask about the man to whom the people of al-Kūfah are pledging their oath of allegiance. Inform him that you are a man from Ḥimṣ who came for this matter, and this is money you give him to strengthen his position."

That servant was gentle and kind until he was directed to an elder from the people of al-Kūfah who was overseeing the pledge. He met him and informed him of his intention. The elder said to him: "Your meeting with me has pleased me and saddened me. What pleased me is what Allah has guided you to, and what saddened me is that our matter has not yet been established." He brought him to him, took the money from him, pledged allegiance to him, and returned to ʿUbayd Allāh and informed him.

When ʿUbayd Allāh ibn Ziyād arrived Muslim moved from the house he was in to the house of Hānī ibn ʿUrwah al-Murādī. Muslim ibn ʿAqīl wrote to al-Ḥusayn ibn ʿAlī informing him of the pledge of twelve thousand from the people of al-Kūfah and ordering him to come. ʿUbayd Allāh said to the nobles of the people of al-Kūfah: "Why do I not see Hānī ibn ʿUrwah among those who came to me?" Muḥammad ibn al-Ashʿath went out to him with some of his people while he was at the door of his house. They said: "The governor has mentioned you and found you slow. Go to him." They continued with him until he rode with them and went until he entered upon ʿUbayd Allāh, and Shurayḥ the judge was with him. When he saw him, he said to Shurayḥ: "A traitor has come to you under his own power." When he greeted him, he said: "O Hānī, where is Muslim?" He said: "I do not know." ʿUbayd Allāh ordered his servant, the one in charge of the money, to go out to him. When Hānī, saw him, he became distraught. He said: "May Allah rectify the governor! By Allah, I did not invite him to my house, but he came and threw himself upon me." He said: "Bring him to me." He said: "By Allah, if he were under my feet, I would not lift them from him." He said: "Bring him closer to me." He was brought closer, and he struck him on his eyebrow, splitting it. Hānī reached for one of the policemen's swords to draw it, but was prevented.

ʿUbayd Allāh said: "Allah has made your blood lawful," so he ordered him to be imprisoned in a side of the palace. And it was said by someone other than Abū Jaʿfar: The one who brought Hānī ibn ʿUrwah to ʿUbayd Allāh ibn Ziyād was ʿAmr ibn al-Ḥajjāj al-Zubaydī: Mention of those who said that: ʿAmr ibn ʿAlī narrated to us, he said: Abū Qutaybah narrated to us, he said: Yūnus ibn Abī Isḥāq narrated to us, from al-ʿAyzār ibn Ḥurayth, he said: ʿUmārah ibn ʿUqbah ibn Abī Muʿayṭ narrated to us that he sat in the assembly of Ibn Ziyād and recited:

> Today I chased wild donkeys
> and I caught one,
> so I slaughtered it.

ʿAmr ibn al-Ḥajjāj al-Zubaydī said to him:

> Truly the donkey you slaughter
> is indeed a treacherous donkey.

ʿUmārah said: "Shall I tell you something more treacherous than all of this! A man whose father was brought as an unbeliever to the Messenger of Allah ﷺ, and he ordered his neck to be struck. He said: 'O Muḥammad, who will take care of the children?' He said: 'The fire.' So you are among the children, and you are in the fire." Ibn Ziyād laughed.

We return to the narration of ʿAmmār al-Duhnī, from Abū Jaʿfar, who related: While Hānī was in this situation when the news reached Madhḥij, there was a commotion at the gate of the palace that ʿUbayd Allāh heard. He said, "What is this?" They said, "Madhḥij." He said to Shurayḥ, "Go out to them and inform them that I have only detained him to question him." He sent a spy from his servants to listen to what Hānī would say. As Shurayḥ passed by Hānī' he said to him, "Fear Allāh, O Shurayḥ, for he is going to kill me." Shurayḥ went out and stood at the gate of the palace and said to the people gathered, "No harm has been done to him; the governor has only detained him to question him." They said, "He is right, there has been no harm to your companion," and they dispersed.

The Killing of Muslim Ibn ʿAqīl

The news reached Muslim, and he called out his slogan, and four thousand people from al-Kūfa gathered with him. He placed his vanguard, organized his right and left flanks, and marched in the center towards ʿUbayd Allāh. ʿUbayd Allāh sent for the notables of al-Kūfa and gathered them with him in the palace. When Muslim marched towards him and reached the gate of the palace, they looked down at their tribes and began to speak to them and turn them back. The companions of Muslim began to slip away until only five hundred remained with him. When darkness fell, those also dispersed.

When Muslim saw that he was left alone, wandering the streets, he came to a door and sat down by it. A woman came out to him, and he said to her, "Give me water to drink." She gave him water, then went inside and stayed as long as Allāh willed. Then she came out and found him still at the door. She said, "O servant of Allāh, your sitting here is suspicious, get up." He said, "I am Muslim ibn ʿAqīl, do you have a place of refuge?" She said, "Yes, come in." Her son was a servant of Muḥammad ibn al-Ashʿath. When the boy learned about him, he went to Muḥammad and informed him. Muḥammad went to ʿUbayd Allāh and informed him. ʿUbayd Allāh sent his chief of police ʿAmr ibn Ḥurayth al-Makhzūmī, along with ʿAbd al-Raḥmān ibn Muḥammad ibn al-Ashʿath to bring him to him. Muslim was unaware of their arrival until the house was surrounded. When Muslim saw that, he went out to them with his sword and fought them. ʿAbd al-Raḥmān granted him safe-conduct, so he surrendered. He was brought to ʿUbayd Allāh, who ordered him to be taken to the top of the palace, where his head was struck off, and his body was thrown to the people. He ordered Hānī' to be dragged to the marketplace and crucified there. Their poet said about that:

> If you do not know what death is,
> look at Hānī' in the market and Ibn ʿAqīl.
> The command of the Imām struck them,
> and they became tales for those who strive by every means.
> Does Asmā' ride the camels safely,
> while Madhḥij seeks him with vengeance?

Abū Mikhnaf's Account of the Killing of Muslim ibn ʿAqīl

As for Abū Mikhnaf, he mentioned the story of Muslim ibn ʿAqīl and his journey to al-Kūfa and his killing, a story that is more detailed and complete than the report of ʿAmmār al-Duhnī from Abū Jaʿfar mentioned before. Hishām ibn Muḥammad related: ʿAbd al-Raḥmān ibn Jundub told me, he said: ʿUqba ibn Samʿān, the servant of al-Rubāb, daughter of Imruʾ al-Qays al-Kalbiyya, wife of Ḥusayn - and she was with Sukayna, daughter of Ḥusayn, and ʿUqba was a servant of her father, and she was young at that time - said: We set out and adhered to the main road. Ḥusayn's family said to him: "If you avoid the main road as Ibn al-Zubayr did, the pursuit will not catch up with you." He said: "No, by Allāh, I will not leave it until Allāh decrees what He loves." We were met by ʿAbd Allāh ibn Muṭīʿ, who said to Ḥusayn: "May I be your ransom! Where are you heading?" He said: "For now, I am heading to Mecca, and after that, I will seek Allāh's guidance." He said: "May Allāh guide you, and may we be your ransom. When you come to Mecca, do not approach al-Kūfa, for it is a cursed town. Your father was killed there, your brother was betrayed, and he was stabbed with a wound that almost took his life. Stay in the sanctuary, for you are the leader of the Arabs. By Allāh, the people of al-Ḥijāz will not prefer anyone over you, and people will come to you from all sides. Do not leave the sanctuary, may my uncle and my maternal uncle be your ransom. By Allāh, if you perish, we will be enslaved after you."

So al-Ḥusayn went on until he settled in Mecca. The people of Mecca began to come to him, as well as the pilgrims who were there and people from afar. Ibn al-Zubayr was there, close to the Kaʿba. He was standing and praying there most of the day and circumambulating the Kaʿba. He would come to Ḥusayn among those who came to him. He would come to him for two consecutive days, and then once every two days. He would constantly advise him, yet he was the most burdensome of Allāh's creation to Ibn al-Zubayr. He knew that the people of al-Ḥijāz would never pledge allegiance to him or follow him while al-Ḥusayn was present in the city. Ḥusayn was greater in their eyes and hearts than him, the people were more obedient to al-Ḥusayn than to him.

The People of al-Kūfa Write to al-Ḥusayn

When the people of al-Kūfa heard of the death of Muʿāwiya, the people of Iraq began to spread rumors about Yazīd, saying:" Ḥusayn and Ibn al-Zubayr have refused to pledge the oath of allegiance and have gone to Mecca."

The people of al-Kūfa wrote to Ḥusayn. Their governor was al-Nuʿmān ibn Bashīr. Abū Mikhnaf related: Al-Ḥajjāj ibn ʿAlī told me, from Muḥammad ibn Bishr al-Hamdānī, he said: The Shīʿa gathered in the house of Sulaymān ibn Ṣurad. We mentioned the death of Muʿāwiya, and we praised Allāh for it. Sulaymān ibn Ṣurad said to us: "Muʿāwiya has died, and Ḥusayn has taken control of the people by withholding his pledge of allegiance. He has gone to Mecca, and you are his Shīʿa and the Shīʿa of his father. If you know that you will support him and fight his enemy, then write to him. If you fear hesitation and failure, do not deceive the man about himself." They said: "No, we will fight his enemy and give our lives for him." He said: "Write to him," so they wrote to him:

> In the name of Allāh, the Most Gracious, the Most Merciful. To Ḥusayn ibn ʿAlī from Sulaymān ibn Ṣurad, al-Musayyib ibn Najba, Rufaʿa ibn Shaddād, Ḥabīb ibn Muẓāhir, and his Shīʿa from the believers and Muslims of al-Kūfa. Peace be upon you. We praise to you Allāh, there is no god but Him. To proceed, praise be to Allāh who has broken your enemy, the tyrant, the stubborn one who seized this nation and usurped its affairs, and took its spoils, and ruled over it without its consent. Then he killed its best and spared its worst, and made the wealth of Allāh circulate among its tyrants and its rich. So away with him, as Thamūd was away! There is no Imām over us, so come, perhaps Allāh will unite us with you on the truth. Al-Nuʿmān ibn Bashīr is in the palace of the emirate; we do not gather with him for Friday prayer, nor do we go out with him for Eid. If we hear that you have come to us, we will expel him until we send him back to al-Shām, if Allāh wills. Peace and Allāh's mercy be upon you.

He said: Then we sent the letter with ʿAbd Allāh ibn Sabʿ al-Hamdānī and ʿAbd Allāh ibn Wāl, and we ordered them to hasten. The two men set out quickly until they arrived at Ḥusayn ten days into the month of Ramadan in

Mecca (June 14, 680 CE). We then waited two days, and then sent to him Qays ibn Mushir al-Ṣaydāwī, ʿAbd al-Raḥmān ibn ʿAbd Allāh ibn al-Kadn al-Arḥabī, and ʿUmāra ibn ʿUbayd al-Salūlī. They carried with them about fifty-three letters, each letter from one, two, or four men.

He said: Then we waited another two days, then we sent to him Hānīʾ ibn Hānīʾ al-Sabīʿī and Saʿīd ibn ʿAbd Allāh al-Ḥatfī, and we wrote with them:

> In the name of Allāh, the Most Gracious, the Most Merciful. To Ḥusayn ibn ʿAlī from his Shīʿa from the believers and Muslims. To proceed, welcome, for the people are waiting for you, and they have no thought of other than you. So, hasten, hasten. Peace be upon you.

Shabath ibn Ribʿī, Ḥijār ibn Abjar, Yazīd ibn al-Ḥārith ibn Yazīd ibn Ruwaym, ʿAzra ibn Qays, ʿAmr ibn al-Ḥajjāj al-Zubaydī, and Muḥammad ibn ʿUmayr al-Tamīmī wrote:

> To proceed, the land has turned green, the fruits have ripened, and the springs have overflowed. If you wish, come to an army ready for you. Peace be upon you.

All the messengers met with him, and he read the letters and asked the messengers about the people's situation. Then he wrote with Hānīʾ ibn Hānīʾ al-Sabīʿī and Saʿīd ibn ʿAbd Allāh al-Ḥanīfī, who were the last messengers:

> In the name of Allāh, the Most Gracious, the Most Merciful. From Ḥusayn ibn ʿAlī to the assembly of the believers and Muslims. To proceed, Hānīʾ and Saʿīd have come to me with your letters, and they were the last of your messengers to come to me. I have understood everything you have recounted and mentioned, and the statement of most of you: "There is no Imām over us, so come, perhaps Allāh will unite us with you on guidance and truth." I have sent to you my brother, my cousin, and my trusted one from my household [Muslim bin ʿAqīl], and I have ordered him to write to me about your condition, your affairs, and your opinions. If he writes to me that the opinion of your notables and those of virtue and wisdom among you is united on what your messengers have brought to me and what I have read in your letters, I will come to

> you soon, if Allāh wills. By my life, the Imām is none other than one who acts according to the Book, upholds justice, adheres to the truth, and dedicates himself to Allāh. Peace be upon you.

Abū Mikhnaf related: Abū al-Mukhāriq al-Rāsibī mentioned that a group of Shīʿa gathered in the house of a woman from ʿAbd al-Qays, named Māriya bint Saʿd - or Munqidh - for several days. She was a Shīʿa supporter, and her house was a meeting place where they would talk. When Ibn Ziyād learned of Ḥusayn's approach, he wrote to his governor in Basra to set up lookouts and and take control of the road. However, Yazīd bin Nabīṭ – from the tribe of ʿAbd al-Qays – decided to leave to join al-Ḥusayn, and he had ten sons, so he said: "Which of you will go with me?" Two of his sons volunteered with him: ʿAbd Allāh and ʿUbayd Allāh, so he said to his companions in the house of that woman [Māriya bint Saʿd]: "I have resolved to leave, and I am leaving", so they said to him: "We fear for you from the companions of Ibn Ziyād," he said: "By God, if the hooves of my she-camels were to settle on the ground, it would be easy for me to be sought by those who seek me."

Then Yazīd bin Nabīṭ left and proceeded on the road until he reached al-Ḥusayn, and he entered his camp at al-Abṭaḥ, and al-Ḥusayn was informed of his arrival, so he searched for him. The man came to the camp of al-Ḥusayn, and it was said to him: "He has gone to your house," he followed him. When al-Ḥusayn did not find him, he sat in his camp waiting for him. The Basran came and found him sitting in his camp, and he said: "*By the grace of God and His mercy, let them rejoice in that.*" (Sūrat Yūnus, 10:59) He greeted him and sat with him, and informed him of what he had come for, so al-Ḥusayn prayed for his well-being. Then he proceeded with him until he came and fought beside him, and Yazīd bin Nabīṭ was killed with him along with his two sons.

Then he called Muslim bin ʿAqīl and sent him with Qays bin Musʿhir al-Ṣaydāwī, ʿAmāra bin ʿUbayd al-Salūlī, and ʿAbd al-Raḥmān bin ʿAbd Allāh bin al-Kadn al-Arḥabī, and he ordered him to fear God, conceal his matter, and be courteous. If he saw the people united and steadfast, he should hasten to inform of that.

Muslim proceeded until he reached al-Madīna and prayed in the mosque of the Messenger of God, and bid farewell to those he loved from his family.

Then he hired two guides from Qays, and they proceeded with him. They lost their way and wandered, and they were severely thirsty. The guides said: "This is the way until you reach the water, and they were about to die of thirst." Muslim bin ʿAqīl wrote with Qays bin Musʿhir al-Ṣaydāwī to Ḥusayn, and that was at the narrow pass of Batin al-Khabīt:

> To proceed, I have come from al-Madīna with two guides, and they have wandered off the path and lost their way, and we were severely thirsty. They did not last long before they died, and we proceeded until we reached the water. We survived only by the skin of our teeth, and that water is at a place called the narrow pass of Batin al-Khabīt. I have become pessimistic about this matter, so if you see fit, relieve me of it and send someone else. Peace.

Al-Ḥusayn ﷺ wrote to him:

> To proceed, I feared that your writing to me to be excused from the mission I sent you on was due to cowardice. Proceed with the mission I sent you on. Peace be upon you.

Muslim said to the one who read the letter: "It is not that I fear for myself," and he continued as he was until he passed by the waterhole of Ṭayy, where he halted. Then he departed from it, and there saw a man hunting. He saw him shoot a gazelle when it appeared before him, bringing it down. Muslim said: "Our enemy will be killed, God willing." Then Muslim continued until he entered Kūfa and stayed at the house of al-Mukhtār bin Abī ʿUbayd—which is today called the house of Muslim bin al-Musayyib. The Shīʿa began to come to him, and when a group of them gathered around him, he read to them the letter of Ḥusayn, and they began to weep.

ʿĀbis bin Abī Shabīb al-Shākirī stood up, praised God, and said:

> To proceed, I do not inform you about the people, nor do I know what is in their hearts, and I do not deceive you about them. By God, I will tell you about what I have resolved for myself. By God, I will answer you when you call, I will fight with you against your enemy, and I will strike with my sword for you until I meet God. I seek nothing but what is with God.

Ḥabīb bin Muẓāhir al-Faqʿasī stood up and said: "May God have mercy on you! You have fulfilled what is in your heart with a few words." Then he said: "By Allah, the One besides whom there is no god, I am upon the same as this." Then al-Ḥanafī said the same. al-Ḥajjāj ibn ʿAlī said: "I asked Muḥammad ibn Bishr: 'Did you say anything?' He said: 'I wished that God would honor my companions with victory, but I did not wish to be killed, and I hated to lie.'

The Shīʿa continued to visit him until his location was known, and this reached the governor al-Nuʿmān ibn Bashīr.

Abū Mikhnaf related: Namīr ibn Waʿla narrated to me from Abū al-Wudāk, who said: al-Nuʿmān ibn Bashīr came out to us, ascended the pulpit, praised God, and said: "To proceed, fear God, servants of God, and do not hasten to discord and division, for in them men perish, blood is shed, and wealth is seized," for he was a gentle, devout man who loved peace.

Al-Nuʿmān ibn Bashīr said:

> I do not fight those who do not fight me, nor do I attack those who do not attack me, nor do I insult you, nor do I provoke you, nor do I act with suspicion or accusation. But if you show your hostility towards me, break your pledge, and oppose your leader, then By Allah, the One besides whom there is no god, I will strike you with my sword as long as its hilt remains in my hand, even if I have no supporter among you. I hope that those who know the truth among you are more than those who are misled by falsehood.

ʿAbd Allāh ibn Muslim ibn Saʿīd al-Ḥaḍramī, ally of Banū Umayya, stood up and said: "What you see will not be resolved except by force. This opinion you hold between you and your enemy is the view of the weak." Al-Nuʿmān replied: "To be among the weak in obedience to God is more beloved to me than to be among the strong in disobedience to God." Then he descended.

ʿAbd Allāh ibn Muslim went out and wrote to Yazīd ibn Muʿāwiya:

> To proceed, Muslim ibn ʿAqīl has arrived in al-Kūfa, and the Shīʿa have pledged allegiance to him for Ḥusayn ibn ʿAlī. If you have

> any need in al-Kūfa, send a strong man who will execute your orders and act as you would against your enemy, for al-Nuʿmān ibn Bashīr is a weak man, or he is weakening.

ʿAbd Allāh ibn Muslim was the first to write to Yazīd. Then ʿAmāra ibn ʿUqba wrote to him similarly, and then ʿUmar ibn Saʿd ibn Abī Waqqāṣ wrote to him in the same manner.

Hishām said: ʿAwāna said: When the letters gathered with Yazīd, with only two days between them, Yazīd ibn Muʿāwiya called Sarjūn, the servant of Muʿāwiya, and said: "What is your opinion? It is reported that Ḥusayn has headed towards al-Kūfa, and Muslim ibn ʿAqīl is in al-Kūfa pledging allegiance to Ḥusayn. I have heard about al-Nuʿmān's weakness and bad speech" - and he read their letters to him – "so what do you think about appointing someone else over al-Kūfa?" Yazīd was displeased with ʿUbayd Allāh ibn Ziyād. Sarjūn said: "If Muʿāwiya were to rise from the grave, would you take his opinion?" He said: "Yes." So he brought out the appointment of ʿUbayd Allāh over al-Kūfa and said: "This is Muʿāwiya's opinion, and he died having ordered this letter." So Yazīd ibn Muʿāwiya took his opinion and combined the two cities under ʿUbayd Allāh, and sent him the letter of appointment over them.

Then he called Muslim ibn ʿAmr al-Bāhilī - who was with him - and sent him to ʿUbayd Allāh with his letter of appointment to al-Baṣra, and wrote to him:

> To proceed, my Shīʿa from the people of al-Kūfa have written to me informing me that ibn ʿAqīl is in al-Kūfa gathering crowds to break the unity of the Muslims. So hasten when you read this letter of mine until you come to the people of al-Kūfa and seek ibn ʿAqīl as you would seek a treasure until you capture him, bind him, kill him, or exile him. Peace be upon you.

Muslim ibn ʿAmr proceeded until he arrived at ʿUbayd Allāh in al-Baṣra. ʿUbayd Allāh ordered preparations and readiness to march to al-Kūfa the next day.

Al- Ḥusayn's Letter to the Basrans

Ḥusayn had written a letter to the people of al-Baṣra. Hishām said: Abū Mikhnaf related: Ṣaqʿab ibn Zuhayr narrated to me from Abū ʿUthmān al-Nahdī, who said: Ḥusayn wrote with a servant of theirs named Sulaymān, and wrote a copy to the heads of the five division in al-Baṣra and to the nobles. He wrote to Mālik ibn Musmaʿ al-Bakrī, to al-Aḥnaf ibn Qays, to al-Mundhir ibn al-Jārūd, to Masʿūd ibn ʿAmr, to Qays ibn al-Haytham, and to ʿAmr ibn ʿUbayd Allāh ibn Maʿmar. One copy came from him to all their nobles:

> To proceed, God has chosen Muḥammad ﷺ over His creation, honored him with His prophethood, and chose him for His message. Then God took him to Himself after he had advised His servants and conveyed what he was sent with ﷺ. We were his family, his allies, his trustees, his heirs, and the most deserving of his position among the people. Our people took that from us, and we accepted it, disliking division, and loving peace. We know that we are more deserving of that rightful position than those who have taken it. They have done well and acted rightly, seeking the truth. May God have mercy on them and forgive us and them.
>
> I have sent my messenger to you with this letter, and I invite you to the Book of Allah and the Sunnah of His Prophet ﷺ. The Sunnah has been extinguished, and innovation has been revived. If you listen to my words and obey my command, I will guide you to the path of righteousness. Peace be upon you and the mercy of God.

Everyone who read that letter from the nobles kept it secret, except for al-Mundhir ibn al-Jārūd, who feared that it might be a trick from ʿUbayd Allāh. He brought the messenger to him in the evening, the night before he intended to leave for al-Kūfa, and read the letter to him. The messenger arrived, and ʿUbayd Allāh had him executed. ʿUbayd Allāh ascended the pulpit in al-Baṣra, praised God, and said:

> To proceed, by Allah, I am not intimidated by difficulties, nor do I fear threats. I am a punishment for those who oppose me and a poison for those who fight me. I am fair to those who challenge

> me. O people of al-Baṣra, the Commander of the Faithful has appointed me over al-Kūfa, and I am leaving for it tomorrow morning. I have appointed ʿUthmān ibn Ziyād ibn Abī Sufyān as my deputy over you. Beware of discord and rumors. By God, who there is no god but Him, if I hear of any opposition from any of you, I will kill him, his leader, and his guardian. I will hold the nearest accountable for the farthest until you listen to me, and there will be no opposition or dissent among you. I am the son of Ziyād, resembling him among those who tread the earth, and no resemblance of an uncle or cousin has taken me away.

Then he left al-Baṣra, appointing his brother ʿUthmān ibn Ziyād as his deputy, and headed towards al-Kūfa with Muslim ibn ʿAmr al-Bāhilī, Sharīk ibn al-Aʿwar al-Ḥārithī, his servants, and his family. He entered al-Kūfa wearing a black turban and veiled, while the people had heard of Ḥusayn's arrival and were awaiting him. They thought that ʿUbayd Allāh was Ḥusayn when he arrived, and greeted him, saying: "Welcome, O son of the Messenger of God! You have come with the best arrival." He saw their joy for Ḥusayn, which displeased him. Muslim ibn ʿAmr said when they crowded around: "Step back, this is the governor ʿUbayd Allāh ibn Ziyād." He arrived at noon with only a few men. When he entered the palace and the people realized that it was ʿUbayd Allāh ibn Ziyād, they felt great sadness and depression. ʿUbayd Allāh was angered by what he heard from them and said: "Do I not see these people as I see?"

Hishām said: Abū Mikhnaf related: al-Muʿallā ibn Kulayb narrated to me from Abū Wadāk, who said: When ʿUbayd Allāh ibn Ziyād entered the palace, it was announced: "The prayer is gathering." The people gathered, and he came out to us, praised God, and said:

> To proceed, the Commander of the Faithful, may God rectify him, has appointed me over your city and your frontier. He has ordered me to be just to the oppressed among you, to give to the deprived among you, to be kind to those who listen and obey among you, and to be harsh on those who are suspicious and disobedient among you. I will follow his instructions concerning you and will carry out his authorization among you. I will show kindness to those who obey him and treated them as a benevolent father. However, for those who disobey or betray me, my sword and whip await them

> as a sign of consequence. Let each man save himself. *Truthfulness should avert evil from you without threat of punishment.*

He then descended. He took stern measures against the tribal leaders and the people, announcing:

> Write down the names of Haruriyyah [a faction of the Khawarij], rebels against the authority of the leader, and those who sought division and discord. Those who cooperate and provide these lists are to be absolved of responsibility. However, those who refused to comply or failed to report, it is lawful for us to take his wealth and shed his blood. Any chieftain found having someone opposing the Commander of the Faithful's authority in their charge without reporting them would face harsh consequences. They would be crucified at the gate of their house, their stipend cut off, and they would be exiled to a remote place, such as Oman Al-Zarah.

As for ʿĪsā ibn Yazīd al-Kinānī, it is narrated by ʿUmar ibn Shabbah, through Hārūn ibn Muslim and ʿAlī ibn Ṣāliḥ, that when Yazīd's letter reached ʿUbayd Allāh ibn Ziyād, a group of 500 individuals, including ʿAbd Allāh ibn al-Ḥārith ibn Nawfal and Sharīk ibn al-Aʿwar (the latter being an ally of ʿAlī ﷺ), were chosen from the people of Basra. Among them, Sharīk fell behind first, followed by ʿAbd Allāh ibn al-Ḥārith, accompanied by others. They hoped that ʿUbayd Allāh would delay his advance so that Ḥusayn could arrive in Kūfa before him. However, ʿUbayd Allāh paid no attention to those who faltered along the way and proceeded until he reached Al-Qādisiyyah. His servant Mehrān collapsed, and ʿUbayd Allāh said, 'Oh Mehrān, if you manage to hold on until you see the palace, I will reward you with one hundred thousand dirhams.' Mehrān replied, 'No, by Allah, I cannot.'

ʿUbayd Allāh dismounted, took out worn-out Yemeni garments, wrapped himself in a Yemeni shawl, mounted his mule, and continued on foot alone. He passed through checkpoints where those who saw him assumed he was Ḥusayn, saying, 'Welcome, O son of the Messenger of Allah!' He remained silent and did not respond. People began to emerge from their homes and gather around him. When Al-Nuʿmān ibn Bashīr heard the commotion, he locked himself and his inner circle inside. ʿUbayd Allāh eventually reached him with a crowd following, all under the impression that he was Ḥusayn.

Al-Nuʿmān addressed him, saying: "In Allah's Name, would you just move away from me! I am not one to entrust my honesty to your care, nor do I have any desire to kill you."

He kept silent and did not respond, then approached and while Al-Nuʿmān leaned over the balcony, still attempting to speak. He said, "Open the gate—may it remain closed forever—for the night has grown long." Someone overheard this and hurried to inform the group, exclaiming, "Oh people, it is Ibn Marjanah, by the One besides whom there is no god!" They replied, "Woe unto you! It is Ḥusayn." Al-Nuʿmān opened the gate for him, allowing him to enter, and the gate was shut against the crowd, causing them to disperse. By morning, he ascended the pulpit and said, "Oh people, I know that those who followed me and feigned loyalty to me were enemies to Ḥusayn, thinking that Ḥusayn had entered the city and taken control. By God, I did not recognize anyone among you." He then stepped down and revealed that Muslim ibn ʿAqīl had arrived the night before and was somewhere near Kūfa. He summoned a servant of the Banū Tamīm and gave him money. He said, "Take up this matter, assist them with money, and approach Hānī and Muslim to settle with them."

The servant then went to Hānī and informed him that he was an ally and had brought funds to support his cause. Sharīk ibn al-Aʿwar, who was unwell, said to Hānī, "Send Muslim to stay with me because ʿUbayd Allāh will visit me soon." Sharīk also asked Muslim, "If I give you an opportunity to strike ʿUbayd Allāh with a sword, will you take it?" Muslim replied, "Yes, by Allah." When ʿUbayd Allāh came to visit Sharīk at Hānī's home—following Sharīk's plan—Sharīk told Muslim, "When you hear me say, 'Bring me water,' come out and attack him." ʿUbayd Allāh sat on Sharīk's bed with Mehrān standing nearby. Sharīk called out, "Bring me water," and a maid approached with a cup but turned away when she saw Muslim. Sharīk repeated, "Bring me water," and added a third time, "Woe unto you! Offer me water even if it costs me my life." This alerted Mehrān, who nudged ʿUbayd Allāh to leave quickly. Sharīk then said, "Oh ruler, I wish to entrust you with my will." He replied, "I will return to you," and Mehrān kept urging him to leave, saying, "By Allah, he intended to kill you." He replied, "How could he, with my honoring of Sharīk and in the house of Hānī, whom my own father treated with great favor!" He returned and sent for Asmāʾ ibn Khārijah and Muḥammad ibn al-Ashʿath, saying, "Bring

Hānī to me." They said to him, "He will not come except with a guarantee of safe conduct." He replied, "What does he need a guarantee of safe conduct for? Has he committed any offense? Go, and if he does not come except with a guarantee, then grant him a guarantee of safe conduct." They went to him and called him, and he said, "If they take me, they will kill me." They continued to persuade him until they convinced him and brought him while ʿUbayd Allāh was delivering the Friday sermon. Hānī sat in the mosque, and was combing his two braids.

When ʿUbayd Allāh finished his prayer, he called out, "Oh Hānī," and Hānī followed him inside, greeted him, and sat. ʿUbayd Allāh said:

> Oh Hānī, do you not know that my father came to this city and left no one from this faction except that he killed them, except for your father and Ḥujr? And you know what happened with Ḥujr. My father continued to treat you well, then wrote to the governor of Kūfa requesting him to treat you well?

Hānī replied, "Yes." ʿUbayd Allāh continued, "And what was my reward? You have hidden in your house a man intending to kill me!" Hānī responded, "I did no such thing." At that moment, the informant from the Tamīm tribe, who had been spying on them, was brought forward. When Hānī saw him, he realized the truth was disclosed. Hānī said, "Oh governor, what you have heard is true, but I will not forget your generosity towards me. You and your family are under my protection; go where you wish." At this, ʿUbayd Allāh faltered, and Mehrān, standing beside him with a staff in his hand, exclaimed, "Oh, what humiliation! This slave of a weaver grants you safe conduct in the place where you are authority!" ʿUbayd Allāh said: "Take him," and he threw down his staff, grabbed Hānī's braids, then slapped his face. Then ʿUbayd Allāh took the staff and struck Hānī's face, and the tip broke off and got stuck in the wall. He then struck his face until he broke his nose and brow.

The people heard the commotion, and the news reached Madhhij tribe, so they came and surrounded the house.

ʿUbayd Allāh ordered Hānī to be thrown into a room, while the Madhhij people cried out. ʿUbayd Allāh ordered Mehrān to bring Shuraiḥ to him, and he went out and brought him in, and the guards entered with him. Hānī said: "O Shuraiḥ, you see what they are doing to me!" He said: I" see you alive." He said: "And I am alive with what you see! Inform my people that if they leave, they will kill me."

So he went out to ʿUbayd Allāh and said: "I have seen him alive, and I have seen marks of harm on him." He said: "Do you deny that the governor punishes his subjects? Go out to these people and inform them." So he went out, and ʿUbayd Allāh ordered a man to go out with him. Shuraiḥ said to them: "What is this bad behavior! The man is alive, and his ruler has reprimanded him with a beating that did not reach taking his life. So disperse and do not give cause for bringing harm to yourselves or your companion." So they dispersed.

Another Report of the Killings of Hānī ibn ʿUrwah al-Murādī and Muslim ibn ʿAqīl

Hishām reported from Abū Mikhnaf, through al-Maʿlā ibn Kulayb, from Abū al-Wadāk, who said: Sharīk ibn al-Aʿwar stayed at the house of Hānī ibn ʿUrwah al-Murādī. Sharīk was a supporter of the Shiʿa cause and had fought at Ṣiffīn alongside ʿAmmār.

When Muslim ibn ʿAqīl [who had already arrived in al-Kufa and settled in the house of Mukhtār] heard about the arrival of ʿUbayd Allāh and his statements, as well as the actions he took against the leaders and the people, he left Mukhtār's house—having learned about him—and proceeded to the house of Hānī ibn ʿUrwah al-Murādī. He entered his door and sent word to him to come out. When Hānī came out, he felt uneasy about Muslim's presence. Muslim then said to him, "I have come to you seeking your protection and hospitality." He replied, "May God have mercy on you! You have placed a great burden upon me. Were it not for your entering my house and placing your trust in me, I would have preferred to ask you to leave. However, my sense of obligation compels me, and it is not fitting for someone like me to turn away someone like you out of ignorance. Enter." So, he sheltered him, and the Shi'a began to gather at the house of Hānī ibn ʿUrwah.

Ibn Ziyād summoned a servant named Ma'qil and said to him: "Take these three thousand dirhams, then seek out Muslim ibn ʿAqīl and his companions. Give them the three thousand dirhams and tell them: 'Use this to aid you in the war against your enemy.' Inform them that you are one of them, for if you give them this money, they will trust you and confide in you, not hiding any of their news from you. Go to visit them early each morning.

Ma'qil did as bidden and came to Muslim ibn ʿAwsaja al-Asadī from the Banū Saʿd ibn Thalabah tribe in the great mosque while he was praying and Ma'qil heard some people saying that this man had pledged al- Ḥusayn. He came and sat beside him until he finished his prayer, then said: "O ʿAbd Allāh, I am a man from the people of Shām, a servant of Dhū al-Kalāʿ, blessed by Allah with love for the People of the House and love for those who love them. Here are three thousand dirhams that I wanted to use to meet a man from them who has come to Kūfa to pledge allegiance to the son of the daughter of the Messenger of Allah ﷺ. I wanted to meet him but could not find anyone to guide me to him or know his location. While I was sitting in the mosque, I heard a group of Muslims saying: 'This man has knowledge of the People of the House.' I have come to you to give you this money and to introduce me to your leader so I can pledge allegiance to him. If you wish, you can take my pledge before meeting him."

Muslim ibn ʿAwsaja said: "I thank Allah for meeting you, as it pleases me to help you achieve what you desire, and may Allah support the people of the Prophet's House through you. It has worried me that you know my involvement in this matter before it has developed, for I fear this tyrant and his harshness."

Before Ma'qil left, he pledged his allegiance [to support Muslim ibn ʿAqīl] and swore himself to be sincere and keep the matter secret and gave him assurances that satisfied him. Then Muslim ibn ʿAwsaja said to him: "Come to my house regularly for a few days, for I will seek permission for you [to visit] our master." So Ma'qil began to come with the people to visit Muslim ibn ʿAwsaja, who sought permission for him to meet [Muslim ibn ʿAqīl].

Hānī ibn ʿUrwa fell ill, and ʿUbayd Allāh Ibn Ziyād came to visit him. ʿAmāra ibn ʿUbayd al-Sulūlī said to him: "Our group and our plan is to kill this tyrant, for God has given you power over him, so kill him." Hānī said: "I do not want him to be killed in my house." Then ʿUbayd Allāh left.

It was not long before Sharīk ibn al-Aʿwar fell ill - and he was dear to Ibn Ziyād and to other governors, and he was a staunch Shīʿa. So ʿUbayd Allāh sent to him: "I am coming to you this evening." So Sharīk said to Muslim: "This wicked man is coming to visit me this evening, so when he sits, go out to him and kill him, then go sit in the palace, no one will come between you and him. If I recover from this illness in these days, I will go to al-Baṣra and take care of its affairs on your behalf."

That evening, ʿUbayd Allāh came to visit Sharīk. Muslim ibn ʿAqīl hid, preparing for him to enter, and Sharīk said to him: "Do not let him escape you when he sits." Hānī ibn ʿUrwa came to Muslim and said: "I do not want him to be killed in my house" - as if he found it distasteful. Then ʿUbayd Allāh ibn Ziyād arrive, entered and sat, then asked Sharīk about his illness saying: "What do you feel?" Sharīk replied, "And when did I complain?" Sharīk prolonged his responses but saw that Muslim would not emerge, and he feared he would miss him, so he began to say: "What are you waiting for? To greet Salmā? Bring water to me, even if it costs me my life." He repeated these lines twice or three times, and ʿUbayd Allāh, unaware of the situation, said: "Do you think he is delirious?" Ḥānī replied: "Yes, may Allāh make you prosper! This has been his state since before dawn until now!" Then ʿUbayd Allāh got up and left, and Muslim emerged afterward.

Sharīk said to Muslim, 'What stopped you from killing him?' Muslim replied: "Two reasons: the first was Ḥānī's dislike of having him killed in his house; the second was a saying attributed to the Prophet: 'Faith restrains treachery, and a believer does not engage in treachery."' Ḥānī said, "By God, if you had killed him, you would have killed an immoral, wicked, disbelieving traitor. But I disliked having him killed in my house."

Sharīk ibn al-Aʿwar lived for three more days after that and then died. Ibn Ziyād led the funeral prayer for him. Later, after the deaths of Muslim and Ḥānī, ʿUbayd Allāh learned that what he had heard from Sharīk during his illness was actually an incitement for Muslim Ibn ʿAqīl to confront and kill him. ʿUbayd Allāh then said, "By God, I will never lead the funeral prayer for an Iraqi again. By God, if it weren't for the grave of Ziyād among them, I would have dug up Sharīk's grave."

Following this Ma'qil, Ibn Ziyād's servant who had infiltrated Ibn ʿAqīl and his companions by offering them money, visited Muslim ibn ʿAwsaja for several days to gain access to Ibn ʿAqīl. Eventually, Muslim ibn ʿAwsaja brought him to Ibn ʿAqīl after the death of Sharīk ibn al-Aʿwar and revealed all the details he had learned. Ibn ʿAqīl accepted his pledge of allegiance and tasked Abū Thamāma al-Ṣāʿidī with collecting the funds brought by Ma'qil. Abū Thamāma, known for handling their finances, purchasing weapons, and supporting one another, was experienced in such matters and was recognized as a respected Arab knight and Shīʿa leader. Meanwhile, Ma'qil continued frequenting them, being the first to arrive and the last to leave, listening to their news and learning their secrets before delivering the information to Ibn Ziyād.

At that time, Hānī regularly visited ʿUbayd Allāh, but when Muslim stayed with him, he stopped these visits and feigned illness, remaining indoors. Ibn Ziyād eventually remarked to his attendants, "Why do I not see Hānī?" They replied, "He is unwell." Ibn Ziyād responded, "Had I known of his illness, I would have visited him."

Abū Mikhnaf narrated that Mujālid ibn Saʿīd told him that ʿUbayd Allāh summoned Muḥammad ibn al-Ashʿath and Asmā' ibn Khārijah. Abū Mikhnaf also reported that al-Ḥasan ibn ʿUqbah al-Murādī mentioned that ʿAmr ibn al-Ḥajjāj al-Zubaydī accompanied them. Furthermore, Abū Mikhnaf relayed through Namīr ibn Waʿlah, quoting Abū al-Waddāk, that Ruʿah, the sister of ʿAmr ibn al-Ḥajjāj, was married to Hānī ibn ʿUrwah and was the mother of Yaḥyā ibn Hānī. When asked about Hānī's absence, they replied, "We don't know, may God grant you well-being."

Ibn Ziyād complained, saying:

> It has reached me that he has recovered, and he is sitting at the door of his house. Confront him and instruct him not to neglect my rights upon him, for I do not wish for someone like him, esteemed among the Arabs, to be ruined in my sight.

So they approached him until they found him sitting at the door of his house in the evening. They said to him, "What prevents you from meeting the governor? He has mentioned you and has said, 'If I knew he was unwell, I would have visited him.'" He replied, "Illness prevents me." They said, "It has been conveyed to him that you sit at the door of your house every evening. He has become impatient, and the delay and estrangement are intolerable to the ruler. We implore you to ride with us!"

Hānī' called for his clothes, dressed, and then summoned a mule to ride. When he approached the palace, his heart seemed to sense some of what was about to transpire, and he spoke to Ḥassān, son of Asmā' ibn Khārijah, saying, "O son of my brother, by God, I am fearful of this man. What do you think?" Ḥassān replied, "Dear uncle, by God, I see nothing to fear for you. You have not given him any excuse against yourself, and you are innocent of any wrongdoing." It is claimed that Asmā' was unaware of the purpose for which 'Ubayd Allāh had summoned him, while Muḥammad was indeed informed. The group entered upon Ibn Ziyād, and he entered with them. Upon his arrival, Ibn Ziyād said, "His own feet have brought the traitor to me."

Ubayd Allāh had recently married Umm Nāfi, the daughter of 'Amārah ibn 'Uqbah, and when Hānī' approached Ibn Ziyād in the presence of Judge Shuraiḥ, he turned towards him and said: "I desire his favor, and he desires my death. Alas for your friend from Murād!" referring to Ibn Ziyād's kind treatment of him and hospitality. Hānī then asked, "What is it, governor?" Ibn Ziyād replied, "Oh Hānī ibn 'Urwah! What are these matters unfolding in your house against the Commander of the Faithful and the general Muslims? You brought Muslim ibn 'Aqīl into your home, gathered weapons and men in the homes around you, and thought this would remain hidden from me!" Hānī responded, "I did not do this, nor is Muslim with me." Ibn Ziyād countered, "Yes, you did." Hānī again denied it, saying, "I did not." Ibn Ziyād insisted, "Indeed, you did." As the argument continued between them and Hānī refused to yield or admit, Ibn Ziyād summoned Ma'qil, the spy, who came and stood before him. Ibn Ziyād asked, 'Do you recognize this man?' Ma'qil replied, 'Yes.' At this moment, Hānī realized that Ma'qil had been a spy amongst them and had disclosed their secrets.

He hesitated in bewilderment for a moment, then his spirit steadied, and he said to him: "Listen to me and believe my words, for by God, I will not lie to you. By Allah, the One besides whom there is no god, I did not invite him to my house, nor did I know anything about his affairs until I saw him sitting at my door. He asked me for refuge, and I was too ashamed to turn him away. I felt an obligation to shelter and host him, so I welcomed him into my home. What you have heard about him is true. If you wish, I will now give you a solemn guarantee that I harbor no ill intent toward you, or I will provide you with a pledge that you can hold until I bring him to you. I will order him to leave my home and go wherever he pleases, thus relieving me of his obligation of protection."

He responded, "No, by God, you will not leave me until you bring him to me." He replied, "No, by God, I will never bring him to you. You expect me to deliver my guest to you so you can kill him!" He said, "By God, you will bring him to me." He replied, "By God, I will not bring him to you."

As the argument persisted between them, Muslim bin ʿAmr al-Bāhilī—who was neither from the people of Shām nor Baṣra but present in Kūfa—intervened and said, "May God preserve the governor! Leave me with him so I may speak to him," Muslim said this after observing the persistence and refusal of Hānī to hand over ibn Aqil. He then asked Hānī, "Come closer so we may speak," and Hānī approached him. They spoke privately, away from Ibn Ziyād, but still in proximity so that Ibn Ziyād could see them. If their voices grew louder, he could hear them; when they lowered their voices, their words were obscured.

Muslim said to Hānī, "I beseech you in the name of God not to bring ruin upon yourself and calamity upon your people and tribe! By God, I value your life too much to see you slain." Hānī, however, believed that his tribe would rise in his defense, considering the circumstances and their bond. Muslim insisted, "Let me assure you that handing him over will not bring disgrace or dishonor upon you. You are merely delivering him to the authorities."

In response, Hānī declared firmly, "By God, I will not hand over my guest while I remain alive, whole, and capable! Even if I were alone without any supporter, I would not yield him without dying for his sake." The dialogue continued, with Muslim pleading and Hānī resolute in his refusal.

Ibn Ziyād heard all that and ordered for Hānī to be brought near him. They brought him and Ibn Ziyād said, "If you do not bring him to me, the flashing swords will surround your house." He replied, "Woe to you! Do you think you can frighten me with the flashing of swords?" He believed that his tribe would protect him. Ibn Ziyād then said, "Bring him closer to me," and they brought him closer. Ibn Ziyād struck his face with a cane, repeatedly hitting his nose, forehead, and cheeks until his nose was broken, blood flowed onto his clothes, and the flesh of his cheeks and forehead was scattered on his beard. He continued to strike him until the cane broke. Hānī reached for the hilt of a sword belonging to one of the guards, but the man resisted and prevented him. Ibn Ziyād said, 'You have become one of the Haruriyah today! You have brought this upon yourself. We are justified in killing you. Take him and throw him into one of the rooms of the house, lock the door, and place a guard over him." They did so.

Asmā' ibn Khārijah then approached Ibn Ziyād and said, "You have betrayed us all day! You ordered us to bring the man to you, and when we did, you smashed his face, spilled his blood on his beard, and claimed you would kill him!" Ibn Ziyād replied, "And you are here!" He ordered him to be seized and shaken, then left him imprisoned.

As for Muḥammad ibn al-Ash'ath, he said, "The tribal chiefs are satisfied with whatever the governor sees fit, whether for or against us. The governor is merely a disciplinarian."

When 'Amr ibn al-Ḥajjāj heard that Hānī had been killed, he approached with the tribe of Madhḥij until they surrounded the palace with a great number of people. He then called out, "I am 'Amr ibn al-Ḥajjāj, and these are the knights and leaders of Madhḥij. We have not renounced our allegiance, nor have we abandoned the community. We have heard that our companion is being killed, and we are greatly distressed by this." It was said to 'Ubayd Allāh, "Madhḥij is at the door." He said to Judge Shuraiḥ, "Go to their companion and look at him, then come out and inform them that he is alive and has not been killed, and that you have seen him." Shuraiḥ entered and looked at him.

Abū Mikhnaf narrated that Ṣaq'ab ibn Zuhayr, quoting 'Abd al-Raḥmān ibn Shuraiḥ who said:

I heard him tell Ismā'īl ibn Ṭalḥah that when he entered upon Hānī, Hānī said with blood dripping down his beard, "O God, O Muslim! Has my tribe been destroyed? Where are the people of faith? Where are the people of the city? They have abandoned me to their enemy and the son of their enemy!" When he heard the commotion at the palace gate and I was going out, he went out and followed me, saying: "O Shuraiḥ, I think these are the voices of Madḥij and my followers among the Muslims. If ten men enter, they will rescue me." So I went out to them with Ḥamīd bin Bukair al-Aḥmarī, sent with me by Ibn Ziyād, who was one of his guards standing by his head. By Allah, if it weren't for his presence with me, I would have conveyed to his companions what he ordered me to do. When I went out to them, I said:

> The governor, when he heard your position and your words about your companion, ordered me to visit him. I came to him and looked at him. He ordered me to meet you and inform you that he is alive and that what you heard about his killing was false.

ʿAmr and his companions [of Madḥij] said: "If he wasn't killed, then praise be to Allah," and they left.

Abū Miḫnaf said: Al-Ḥajjāj bin ʿAlī told me, from Muḥammad bin Biṣr al-Hamdānī, he said: When ʿUbayd Allah struck Hānī and imprisoned him, he feared that people would rise against him. He went out and ascended the pulpit in front of the nobles, his guards, and his entourage. He praised Allah and then said: 'O people, adhere to the obedience of Allah and your leaders. Do not differ and do not divide, lest you perish, be humiliated, killed, and deprived. Your brother is a truthful advisor to you, and he has warned you so pay heed.' Then as he started to descend, from the pulpit when the lookouts in the market entered the, running and saying: 'Muslim Ibn ʿAqīl has come! Ibn ʿAqīl has come!' ʿUbayd Allah entered the palace quickly and locked its gates.

Muslim Ibn ʿAqīl Responds to the Killing of Hānī ibn ʿUrwa

Abū Miḫnaf said: "Yūsuf bin Yazīd told me, from ʿAbd Allah bin Ḫāzim, he said:

By Allah, I am the messenger of Ibn ʿAqīl to the palace to see what happened to Hānī. He said: When he was struck and imprisoned, I rode my horse and was the first of the household to enter upon Muslim bin ʿAqīl with the news. And there were women of Murād gathered, crying: 'O my misfortune! O my bereavement!' I entered upon Muslim bin ʿAqīl with the news, and he ordered me to call out to his companions, who had filled the houses around him. Eighteen thousand had pledged allegiance to him, and there were four thousand men in the houses. He said to me: "Call out: 'O victorious ones, kill!' [the battle cry of the Companions of Badr] So I called out: 'O victorious ones, kill!' And the people of Kūfa gathered to him.

Muslim appointed ʿUbayd Allah bin ʿAmr bin ʿAzīz al-Kindī over the quarter of Kinda and Rabiʿa. He said: "March ahead of me with the cavalry." Then he appointed Muslim bin ʿAwsaja al-Asadī over the quarter of Maḏḥij and Asad, and he said: "Dismount among the men, for you are appointed over them." He appointed Abū Ṯumāma al-Ṣāʾidī over the quarter of Tamīm and Hamdān, and he appointed ʿAbbās bin Jaʿda al-Jadalī over the quarter of the city. Then he approached the palace, and when Ibn Ziyād heard of his approach, he took precautions in the palace and locked the gates. Abū Miḫnaf said: "Yūnus bin Abī Isḥāq told me, from ʿAbbās al-Jadalī, he said: We went out with Ibn ʿAqīl, four thousand of us, but by the time we reached the palace, we were only three hundred."

He said: "Muslim advanced among the people of Murād until he surrounded the palace. Then the people called out to us and gathered. By Allah, we did not wait long until the mosque and the market were filled with people. They continued to gather until the evening, and ʿUbayd Allah became distressed. His main concern was to hold the palace gate, and he had only thirty guards, twenty nobles, his family, and his servants with him. The nobles came to Ibn Ziyād from the gate that faced the Roman quarter. Those in the palace with Ibn Ziyād looked out at them, fearing they would be pelted with stones and cursed and the crowd did not stop cursing ʿUbayd Allah and his father. ʿUbayd Allah called Kaṯīr bin Ṣihāb bin al-Ḥuṣayn al-Ḥāriṯī and ordered him to go out with those who obeyed him from Maḏḥij, to march through Kūfa, and discourage the people from supporting Ibn ʿAqīl, to frighten them with war, and warn them of the punishment of the ruler. He ordered Muḥammad bin al-Aṣʿaṯ to go out with those who obeyed him from Kinda and Ḥaḍramawt, to raise a banner of safe-conduct for those who came to him. He said the same to al-Qaʿqāʿ bin Ṣūr al-Ḏuhlī, Ṣabāṯ bin Ribʿī al-Tamīmī, Ḥiğğār bin Abğar al-ʿAğlī, and Ṣimr bin Ḏī al-Ğawṣan al-ʿĀmirī. He kept the rest of the nobles with him, feeling uneasy due to the small number of people with him. Kaṯīr bin Ṣihāb went out to discourage the people from supporting Ibn ʿAqīl."

Abū Miḫnaf said: "Abū Janāb al-Kalbī told me that Kaṯīr found a man from Kalb named ʿAbd al-Aʿlā bin Yazīd, who had worn his weapon intending to go to Ibn ʿAqīl in the quarter of Banī Fatīān. He seized him and then brought him to Ibn Ziyād and informed him of his news. He said to Ibn Ziyād: "I only intended to come to you." He said: "Definitely! You had promised me that from yourself." Then he ordered him to be imprisoned.

Muḥammad bin al-Aṣʿat̲ went out until he stood at the houses of Banī ʿAmāra. ʿAmāra bin Ṣalh̲ab al-Azdī came to him, intending to go to Ibn ʿAqīl, wearing his weapon. He seized him and sent him to Ibn Ziyād, who imprisoned him.

Ibn ʿAqīl sent from the mosque to Muḥammad bin al-Aṣʿat̲ ʿAbd al-Raḥmān bin Ṣuraiḥ al-Ṣabāmī. When Muḥammad bin al-Aṣʿat̲ saw the large number of people who came to him, he began to withdraw and retreat. He sent al-Qaʿqāʿ bin Ṣūr al-D̲uhlī to Muḥammad bin al-Aṣʿat̲: "I have driven Ibn ʿAqīl away from the commotion." So he retreated from his position and approached until he entered upon Ibn Ziyād from the Roman quarter. When Kat̲īr bin Ṣihāb, Muḥammad, and al-Qaʿqāʿ gathered with those who obeyed them from their people, Kat̲īr said to him - they were advisors to Ibn Ziyād: "May Allah rectify the governor! You have many people in the palace from the nobles, your guards, your family, and your servants. Let us go out to them." ʿUbayd Allah refused. He appointed Ṣabāt̲ bin Ribʿī with a banner and sent him out. The people stayed with Ibn ʿAqīl, chanting and gathering until the evening, and their situation was severe. ʿUbayd Allah sent to the nobles and gathered them to him. Then he said: "Look out over the people and promise the obedient ones increase and honor, and frighten the disobedient ones with deprivation and punishment. Inform them of the arrival of the troops from Syria."

Abū Mih̲naf said: "Sulaymān bin Abī Rāṣid told me, from ʿAbd Allah bin H̲āzim al-Kat̲īrī from al-Azd, from Banī Kat̲īr, he said:

The nobles looked out over us. Kat̲īr bin Ṣihāb spoke first until the sun was about to set. He said: "O people, return to your families, do not hasten evil, and do not expose yourselves to killing. These are the troops of the Commander of the Faithful Yazīd who have arrived, and the governor has given Allah a covenant:

> If you continue the war against him and do not withdraw by tonight, he will deprive your offspring of the stipend, disperse your fighters in the campaigns of the people of Syria without any

> provision, and take the innocent with the sick, and the present with the absent, until there remains no remnant of disobedient people among you except that he will taste its consequence."

When the nobles spoke in a similar manner, the people began to disperse and leave when they heard their words.

Abū Miḫnaf said: Al-Mujālid bin Saʿīd told me that the woman would come to her son or brother and say: "Leave, the people are enough for you." And the man would come to his son or brother and say: "Tomorrow the people of Syria will come to you, what will you do with war and evil? Leave," and he would go with him.

They continued to disperse and break up until Ibn ʿAqīl was left with only thirty people. When he saw that evening had come and he had only those few people with him, he went out heading towards the gates of Kinda. He reached the gates with ten of them, then he went out of the gate and found no one with him. He turned around and saw that he could not feel anyone to guide him on the way, or to show him a house, or to support him if an enemy appeared.

Ibn ʿAqīl wandered in the alleys of Kūfa not knowing where to go until he reached the houses of Banī Jubala from Kinda. He walked until he reached the door of a woman named Ṭuʿa - a freedwoman of al-Aṣʿaṯ bin Qays, who had freed her, and she married Usayd al-Ḥaḍramī and bore him Bilāl. Bilāl had gone out with the people, and his mother was standing waiting for him. Ibn ʿAqīl greeted her, and she returned the greeting. He said to her: 'O servant of Allah, give me water to drink.' She went in and brought him water. He sat down, and she took the vessel back inside. Then she came out and said: 'O servant of Allah, did you not drink?' He said: 'Yes.' She said: 'Then go to your family.' He remained silent. She returned and said the same thing, and he remained silent. Then she said to him: 'For Allah's sake, O servant of Allah, go to your family, may Allah protect you. It is not appropriate for you to sit at my door, and I do not permit it.' He stood up and said: 'O servant of Allah, I have no house or tribe in this city. Do you have any reward and kindness, and perhaps I will repay you for it after today?' She said: 'O servant of Allah, what is that?' He said: 'I am Muslim bin ʿAqīl. These people have lied to me and deceived me.' She said: 'You are Muslim!' He said: 'Yes.' She said: 'Enter.'

She brought him into a room in her house other than the one she was in, and she spread a mat for him. She offered him dinner, but he did not eat. It was not long before her son came and saw her frequently entering and leaving the room. He said: 'By Allah, your frequent entering and leaving this room since tonight makes me suspicious! You have something going on.' She said: 'O my son, leave this matter.' He said to her: 'By Allah, you will tell me.' She said: 'Mind your own business and do not ask me about anything.' He insisted, and she said: 'O my son, do not tell anyone what I tell you,' and she made him swear oaths. He swore to her, and she told him. He went to bed and remained silent. Some claimed that he had been estranged from the people, and some said he was drinking with his companions that night.

When the night grew long for Ibn Ziyād, and he no longer heard the voices of Ibn ʿAqīl's companions as he had before, he said to his companions: 'Look out and see if you see any of them!' They looked out and saw no one. He said: 'Look, perhaps they are hiding under the shadows, waiting for you.' They searched the mosque, lowering torches in their hands, and sometimes the light would show them what they wanted, and sometimes it would not. They lowered lanterns and half-burnt torches tied with ropes, then lowered them until they reached the ground. They did this in the farthest and nearest shadows and in the middle, until they did it in the shadow where the pulpit was. When they saw nothing, they informed Ibn Ziyād.

He opened the door of the mosque and went out, ascending the pulpit. His companions went out with him, and he ordered them to sit around him before the night prayer. He ordered ʿAmr bin Nāfiʿ to call out: 'The protection is lifted from any man of the police, the leaders, or the fighters who does not pray the night prayer in the mosque.' It was not long before the mosque was filled with people. Then he ordered his the *muʾadhdhin* was instructed to pronounce the *iqāmah.*

Ḥuṣayn bin Tamīm said: 'If you wish, I will lead the people in prayer, or someone else will lead them, and you will pray in the palace. I do not trust that one of your enemies will not assassinate you!' He said: 'Order my guards to stand behind me as they used to, and circulate among them, for I will not enter if I do not.'

He led the people in prayer, then he stood up, praised Allah, and said: 'To proceed, Ibn ʿAqīl, the foolish and ignorant, has done what you have seen of discord and division. The protection of Allah is lifted from any man we find in his house, and whoever brings him will have his blood money. Fear Allah, servants of Allah, and adhere to your obedience and allegiance, and do not give yourselves a way.' He said: 'O Ḥuṣayn bin Tamīm! May your mother be bereaved of you if a caller calls at a street of the streets of al-Kūfa, or this man goes out and you do not bring him to me. I have given you authority over the houses of the people of al-Kūfa, so send watchers at the mouths of the streets, and tomorrow morning search the houses and inspect them until you bring me this man.

Al-Ḥuṣayn bin Tamīm was in charge of his police, and he was from Banū Tamīm. Then Ibn Ziyād descended and entered, having appointed ʿAmr ibn Ḥurayth as a leader and ordered him over the people. When morning came, he sat in his place and gave permission for the people to enter upon him. Muḥammad ibn al-Ashʿath approached and said: "Welcome to the one whose leadership is not doubted!" Then Ibn Ziyād seated him beside him. The son of that old woman whose mother had sheltered Ibn ʿAqīl, was Bilāl ibn Asīd, who went to ʿAbd al-Raḥmān ibn Muḥammad ibn al-Ashʿath and informed him of Ibn ʿAqīl's hiding at his mother's home. He said: "ʿAbd al-Raḥmān went to his father while he was with Ibn Ziyād and whispered to him." Ibn Ziyād said to him: "What did he tell you?" He said: "He informed me that Ibn ʿAqīl is hiding in one of our houses." Ibn Ziyād prodded him with a stick in his side and said: "Get up and bring him to me immediately."

Abū Mikhnaf related: Qudāmah ibn Saʿīd ibn Zāʾidah ibn Qudāmah al-Thaqafī told me that when Ibn al-Ashʿath stood to bring Ibn ʿAqīl, he sent to ʿAmr ibn Ḥurayth, who was in the mosque, his deputy over the people, to send with Ibn al-Ashʿath sixty or seventy men, all from Qays. He disliked sending his own people with him because he knew that every people dislike Ibn ʿAqīl being found by them. So he sent with him ʿAmr ibn ʿUbayd Allāh ibn ʿAbbās al-Sulamī with sixty or seventy men from Qays.

The Capture of Muslim Ibn ʿAqīl

When they reached the house where Ibn ʿAqīl was, and he heard the sound of horses' hooves and men's voices, he knew that he had been approached. He went out to them with his sword, and they stormed the house. He attacked them, striking them with his sword until he drove them out of the house. Then they returned, and he attacked them again. He and Bukayr ibn Ḥumrān al-Aḥmarī exchanged two blows. Bukayr struck Muslim's mouth, cutting his upper lip and thrusting the sword into the lower lip, knocking out two of his teeth. Muslim struck him a severe blow on the head and followed it with another on the shoulder, almost reaching his chest. When they saw that, they looked down on him from the roof of the house and began to stone him and set fire to bundles of reeds, and threw them down on him from above the house.

When Ibn ʿAqīl saw that, he went out to them with his sword drawn in the alley and fought them. Muḥammad ibn al-Ashʿath approached him and said: "O young man, you have a guarantee of safe conduct, so do not kill yourself [by fighting]." He continued to fight them while saying:

> I swear I will not be killed except as a free man
> And if I see death as something abhorrent
> Every person will one day meet evil
> And mix the cold with the hot and the bitter
> Return the sun's rays and settle
> I fear that I might lie or be deceived.

Muḥammad ibn al-Ashʿath said to him: "You do not lie, nor deceive, nor are you deceived. The people are your cousins, and they will not kill you or harm you." Finally he was overwhelmed by their stones, unable to fight, and exhausted. He leaned his back against the side of that house. Muḥammad ibn al-Ashʿath approached him and said: "You have a guarantee of safe conduct." He said: "Am I safe?" He said: "Yes. The people said: "You are safe," except for ʿAmr ibn ʿUbayd Allāh ibn al-ʿAbbās al-Sulamī, who said: "I have no interest in this matter," and withdrew.

Ibn ʿAqīl said: "If you had not given me a guarantee of safe conduct, I would not have placed my hand in yours." They brought a mule and he was mounted on it. They gathered around him and took his sword from his neck. At that moment, he seemed to despair of his life, and his eyes filled with tears. Then he said: "This is the beginning of treachery." Muḥammad ibn al-Ashʿath said: "I hope there will be no harm upon you." He said: "It is only a hope. Where is your guarantee of safety? Indeed, we belong to Allah and to Him we shall return!" And he wept.

ʿAmr ibn ʿUbayd Allāh ibn al-ʿAbbās said to him: "Whoever seeks what you seek, if what has befallen you befalls him, does not weep."

He said:

> By Allah, I do not weep for myself, nor do I pity myself for being killed, even though I did not wish for a moment to be destroyed. But I weep for my family who are coming to me. I weep for Ḥusayn and the family of Ḥusayn!

Then he turned to Muḥammad ibn al-Ashʿath and said:

> O ʿAbd Allāh, I see that you, by Allah, will be unable to fulfill my oath of safe conduct. Do you have any good in you? Can you send someone from your side to convey a message to Ḥusayn on my behalf, for I do not see him except that he has set out towards you today, or he will set out tomorrow with his family. What you see of my distress is because of that. Tell him: "Indeed, Ibn ʿAqīl sent me to you, and he is in the hands of the people as a prisoner. He does not see it fit that you should proceed to be killed. He says: 'Return with your family, and do not be deceived by the people of al-Kūfa, for they are the companions of your father who used to wish for separation from them by death or killing. Indeed, the people of al-Kūfa have lied to you and lied to me, and there is no valid opinion for a liar.'"

Ibn al-Ashʿath said: "By Allah, I will do it, and I will inform Ibn Ziyād that I have granted you safety."

Abū Mikhnaf related: Jaʿfar ibn Ḥudhayfah al-Ṭāʾī told me - and Saʿīd ibn Shaybān knew the narration - he said: Muḥammad ibn al-Ashʿath called Iyās ibn al-ʿAthl al-Ṭāʾī from Banū Mālik ibn ʿAmr ibn Thumāmah, and he was a poet, and he was a visitor of Muḥammad. He said to him: "Meet Ḥusayn and deliver this letter to him." He wrote in it what Ibn ʿAqīl had ordered him, and said to him: "This is your provision and your equipment, and a gift for your family." Iyās said: "Where can I get a mount, for my mount is exhausted?" He said: "This is a mount, ride it with its saddle."

Then he went out and met him at Zubālah after four nights, informed him of the news, and delivered the message. Ḥusayn said to him: "Everything that is destined will happen, and we find contentment for ourselves and the corruption of our nation, with Allah."

Muslim ibn ʿAqīl, when he moved to the house of Hānī ibn ʿUrwah and eighteen thousand people pledged allegiance to him, sent a letter to Ḥusayn with ʿĀbis ibn Abī Shabīb al-Shākirī:

> To proceed, the scout does not lie to his people. Eighteen thousand people from the people of al-Kūfa have pledged allegiance to me, so hasten to come when my letter reaches you, for all the people are with you, and they have no opinion or inclination towards the family of Muʿāwiyah. Peace be upon you.

Muḥammad ibn al-Ashʿath brought Ibn ʿAqīl to the palace gate, sought permission, and was granted it. He informed ʿUbayd Allāh of the news of Ibn ʿAqīl and how Bukayr struck him. He said: "Away with him!" Muḥammad ibn al-Ashʿath informed him of what had happened and of his granting him safe conduct. ʿUbayd Allāh said: "What do you have to do with safe conduct! Did we send you to grant him safe conduct? We sent you to bring him to us." He fell silent, and Ibn ʿAqīl reached the palace gate, thirsty. At the palace gate, there were people sitting, waiting for permission, among them ʿAmārah ibn ʿUqbah ibn Abī Muʿayṭ, ʿAmr ibn Ḥurayth, Muslim ibn ʿAmr, and Kathīr ibn Shihāb.

Abū Mikhnaf related: Qudāmah ibn Saʿd told me that when Muslim ibn ʿAqīl reached the palace gate, he was thirsty. He reached the palace gate and found a cold jug placed at the gate. Ibn ʿAqīl said: "Give me a drink from this water." Muslim ibn ʿAmr said to him: "Do you see how cold it is! By Allah, you will not taste a drop of it until you taste the boiling water in the fire of Hell!" Ibn ʿAqīl said to him: "Woe to you! Who are you?" He said: "I am the son of the one who recognized the truth when you denied it, advised his leader when you deceived him, and listened and obeyed when you disobeyed and opposed. I am Muslim ibn ʿAmr al-Bāhilī."

Ibn ʿAqīl said: "May your mother be bereaved of you! How harsh, rough, and hard-hearted you are! You, O son of Bāhilah, are more deserving of the boiling water and eternal abode in the fire of Hell than I am." Then he sat leaning against a wall.

Abū Mikhnaf related: Qudāmah ibn Saʿd told me that ʿAmr ibn Ḥurayth sent a servant named Sulaymān, who brought him water in a jug and gave him a drink.

Abū Mikhnaf related: Saʿīd ibn Mudrik ibn ʿAmārah told me that ʿAmārah ibn ʿUqbah sent a servant named Qays, who brought him a jug with a cloth on it and a cup, and poured water into it, then gave him a drink. Every time he drank, the cup filled with blood. When he filled the cup for the third time and went to drink, his two front teeth fell into it. He said: "Praise be to Allah! If it were in my decree for me to drink, I would have drunk it."

Muslim was brought to Ibn Ziyād and did not greet him with the title of governor. The guard said to him: "Will you not greet the governor?" He said to him: "If he intends to kill me, what is the point of my greeting him? And if he does not intend to kill me, then by my life, I will greet him many times." Ibn Ziyād said to him: "By my life, you will be killed." He said: "Is that so?" He said: "Yes." He said: "Then let me make a will to some of my people."

He looked at the companions of ʿUbayd Allāh and saw among them ʿUmar ibn Saʿd [ibn Abi Waqqas]. He said: "O ʿUmar, there is kinship between you and me, and I have a need for you, and it is a secret." ʿUmar refused to let him mention it. ʿUbayd Allāh said to him: "Do not refuse to consider the need of your cousin." He went to him and sat where Ibn Ziyād could see him. Muslim said to him:

> I have a debt in al-Kūfa that I borrowed since I came to al-Kūfa, seven hundred dirhams, so pay it on my behalf, and look after my body, and ask Ibn Ziyād to give it to you, so you can bury it, and send someone to Ḥusayn to turn him back, for I have written to him informing him that the people are with him, and I do not see him except coming.

ʿUmar said to Ibn Ziyād: "Do you know what he said to me? He mentioned such and such." Ibn Ziyād said to him:

> The trustworthy one would not betray you, but the treacherous may be confided in. As for your money, it is yours, and we do not prevent you from doing with it what you like. As for Ḥusayn, if he does not come to us, we will not go to him, and if he comes to us, we will not hold back from him. As for his body, we will not accept your intercession for it, for he is not worthy of that from us. He has fought against us, opposed us, and strived for our destruction.

And they claimed that he said: "As for his body, we do not care what is done with it after we have killed him." Then Ibn Ziyād said: "Oh, son of ʿAqīl! You came to the people when their affairs were united, and their word was one, to scatter them, divide their word, and incite some of them against others!" He said: "No, I did not come for that, but the people of the city claimed that your father killed their best, shed their blood, and acted among them like Khosrow and Caesar. So we came to command justice and call to the rule of the Book."

He said: "And what do you have to do with that, you wicked one! Were we not acting upon that among them while you were in Medina drinking wine!"

He said:

> I drink wine?! By Allah, Allah knows that you are not truthful, and that you spoke without knowledge, and I am not as you mentioned. The one who is more deserving of drinking wine than me is the one who wallows in the blood of Muslims, kills the soul that Allah has forbidden to be killed, kills the soul without a soul, sheds forbidden blood, kills out of anger, enmity, and bad suspicion, and he plays and amuses himself as if he did nothing.

Ibn Ziyād said to him: "You wicked one, your soul is promising you what Allah has prevented, and your people did not see you fit."

He said: "Who are his people, O son of Ziyād?" He said: "The Commander of the Faithful, Yazīd." He said: "Praise be to Allah in every situation, we are content with Allah as a judge between us and you." He said: "It is as if you think you have something in the matter!" He said: "By Allah, it is not a thought, but certainty." He said: "May Allah kill me if I do not kill you in a way that no one has been killed in Islam!" He said:

> Indeed, you are more deserving of introducing into Islam innovations that were not in it. Indeed, you do not leave the evil of killing, the ugliness of mutilation, the wickedness of conduct, and the baseness of domination, and no one among the people is more deserving of it than you.

Ibn Sumayyah [Ibn Ziyād] approached him, cursing him, cursing Ḥusayn, ʿAlī, and ʿAqīl, and Muslim did not speak to him. The people of knowledge claimed that ʿUbayd Allāh ordered water for him, and he was given water in a shard. Then he said to him:

> Only our unwillingness for you to obtain protection by offering you to drink prevented us from offering you to drink because we dislike that you be deprived of drinking. That is why we offered your drink in this way.

Then Ibn Ziyād said: "Take him up to the top of the palace and strike his neck, then follow his body with his head."

Ibn ʿAqīl' said: "O son of al-Ashʿath, by Allah, if you had not given me a promise of safe conduct, I would not have surrendered. Defend me with your sword, for you have broken your covenant."

Then Ibn ʿAqīl said: "O son of Ziyād, by Allah, if there were kinship between you and me, you would not have killed me." Ibn Ziyād retorted: "Where is the one who struck Ibn ʿAqīl's head with the sword and his shoulder?" He was called, and he said: "Go up and be the one who strikes his neck." He went up with him while he was glorifying Allah, seeking forgiveness, and sending prayers on Allah's angels and messengers, saying: "O Allah, judge between us and a people who deceived us, lied to us, and humiliated us. He was brought to the place of the butchers today!" His neck was struck, and his body followed his head.

Abū Mikhnaf related: Ṣaqʿab ibn Zuhayr told me, from ʿAwn ibn Abī Juḥayfah, he said: Bukayr ibn Ḥumrān al-Aḥmarī, who killed Muslim, descended. Ibn Ziyād said to him: "Did you kill him?" He said: "Yes He said: "What was he saying while you were taking him up?" He said: "He was glorifying Allah, praising the Prophet, and seeking forgiveness. When I brought him close to kill him, he said: 'O Allah, judge between us and a people who lied to us, deceived us, abandoned us, and killed us.' I said to him: 'Come closer to me, praise be to Allah who avenged me from you.' I struck him a blow but that did not suffice. He said: 'Do you not see in the scratch you scratched me a fulfillment of your blood, O servant!' Ibn Ziyād said: "Pride even in the face of death!" He said: "Then I struck him a second blow and killed him."

The Execution of Hānī ibn ʿUrwah

Muḥammad ibn al-Ashʿath went to ʿUbayd Allāh ibn Ziyād and spoke to him about Hānī ibn ʿUrwah, saying: "You know the status of Hānī ibn ʿUrwah in the city, and his house in the tribe, and his people know that I and my companion brought him to you. I beseech you by Allah to grant him to me, for I dislike the enmity of his people, they are the most honored people of the city, and the number of the people of Yemen!"

He promised to do so, but when the matter of Muslim ibn ʿAqīl occurred, he changed his mind and refused to fulfill his promise.

He ordered Hānī ibn ʿUrwah to be taken out to the market and his neck to be struck. He was taken out until he reached a place in the market where sheep were sold, and he was bound. He began to say: "O Madhḥaj! There is no Madhḥaj for me today! O Madhḥaj, where is Madhḥaj from me!" When he saw that no one was helping him, he extracted his hand from the bonds, then said: "Is there no stick, knife, stone, or bone with which a man can defend himself?" They jumped at him and tied him up again. Then they said to him: "Extend your neck." He said: "I am not generous with it, nor will I assist you in killing myself."

His neck was struck by a servant of ʿUbayd Allāh ibn Ziyād - a Turk named Rashīd - with a sword, but the sword did nothing. Hānī said: "To Allah is the return! O Allah, to Your mercy and pleasure!" Then he struck him again and killed him.

ʿAbd al-Raḥmān ibn al-Ḥuṣayn al-Murādī saw him at Khāzir, and he was with ʿUbayd Allāh ibn Ziyād. The people said: This is the killer of Hānī ibn ʿUrwah. Ibn al-Ḥuṣayn said: "May Allah kill me if I do not kill him or be killed for him!" He charged at him with a spear and stabbed him, killing him.

When ʿUbayd Allāh ibn Ziyād killed Muslim ibn ʿAqīl and Hānī ibn ʿUrwah, he summoned ʿAbd al-Aʿlā al-Kalbī, who had been captured by Kathīr ibn Shihāb in Banū Fityān. He was brought to him, and he said to him: "Tell me about your matter." He said: "May Allah rectify you! I went out to see what the people were doing, and Kathīr ibn Shihāb captured me." He said to him: "Swear by Allah, with severe oaths, that you did not go out except for what you claimed!" He refused to swear. ʿUbayd Allāh said: "Take him to the cemetery of al-Sabīʿ and strike his neck there." He was taken and his neck was struck.

ʿAmārah ibn Ṣalḥab al-Azdī, who wanted to come to support Muslim ibn ʿAqīl, was also brought to ʿUbayd Allāh. He said to him: "Who are you?" He said: "From al-Azd." He said: "Take him to his people and strike his neck among them."

ʿAbd Allāh ibn al-Zubayr al-Asadī said about the killers of Muslim ibn ʿAqīl and Hānī ibn ʿUrwah al-Murādī—and it is said that al-Farazdaq said it:

> If you do not know what death is,
> then look at Hānī in the market and Ibn ʿAqīl
> To a hero whose face was smashed by the sword
> And another falling from the top, killed
> They were struck by the command of the leader
> and became
> Stories for those who travel on every path
> You see a body whose color has been changed by death
> And blood has flowed from every vein
> A young man who is more alive than a shy girl
> And more cutting than one with two sharp blades
> Will Asmāʾ ride the camels safely
> While Madhḥaj seeks him with vengeance!
> Murād circles around him, and all of them.

Are on his neck, asking and questioning
If you do not avenge your brother
Then be the prostitutes who are satisfied with little"

Letters between ʿUbayd Allāh ibn Ziyād and Yazīd ibn Muʿāwiyah

Abū Mikhnaf related: From Abū Janāb Yaḥyā ibn Abī Ḥayyah al-Kalbī, he said: Then ʿUbayd Allāh ibn Ziyād, after killing Muslim and Hānī, sent their heads with Hānī ibn Abī Ḥayyah al-Wādiʿī and al-Zubayr ibn al-Arwaḥ al-Tamīmī to Yazīd ibn Muʿāwiyah. He ordered his scribe ʿAmr ibn Nāfiʿ to write to Yazīd ibn Muʿāwiyah about what had happened with Muslim and Hānī. He wrote him a lengthy letter - he was the first to write lengthy letters. When ʿUbayd Allāh ibn Ziyād looked at it, he disliked it and said: What is this lengthiness and these superfluities? Write:

> To proceed, praise be to Allah who has taken the right of the Commander of the Faithful and relieved him of the burden of his enemy. Inform the Commander of the Faithful, may Allah honor him, that Muslim ibn ʿAqīl sought refuge in the house of Hānī ibn ʿUrwah al-Murādī. I placed spies over them, sent men to them, and plotted against them until I extracted them. Allah enabled me to capture them, so I brought them forward and struck their necks. I have sent their heads to you with Hānī ibn Abī Ḥayyah al-Hamdānī and al-Zubayr ibn al-Arwaḥ al-Tamīmī - they are people of hearing, obedience, and advice. Let the Commander of the Faithful ask them about whatever he wishes, for they have knowledge, truthfulness, understanding, and piety. Peace be upon you.

Yazīd wrote to him:

> To proceed, you have not failed to be as I desired. You acted with the decisiveness of the resolute and struck with the courage of the steadfast. You have sufficed and fulfilled, and you have confirmed my expectations and my opinion of you. I have summoned your two messengers, questioned them, and conversed with them. I found them in their opinions and virtues as you described. Treat them well. It has reached me that al-Ḥusayn ibn ʿAlī has headed towards Iraq. Place lookouts and guards, be cautious of suspicion,

> and take precautions against accusations. Do not kill anyone except those who fight you. Write to me about everything that happens. Peace be upon you and the mercy of Allah."

"Abū Mikhnaf related: Ṣaqʿab ibn Zuhayr told me, from ʿAwn ibn Abī Juḥayfah, he said: Muslim ibn ʿAqīl's departure from al-Kūfa was on Tuesday, eight nights past from Dhū al-Ḥijjah in the year sixty - and it is said on Wednesday, seven nights past in the year sixty from the day of ʿArafah after al-Ḥusayn's departure from Mecca heading towards al-Kūfa by a day. He said: And al-Ḥusayn's departure from al-Madīnah to Mecca was on Sunday, two nights remaining from Rajab in the year sixty, and he entered Mecca on the night of Friday, three nights past from Shaʿbān. He stayed in Mecca during Shaʿbān, the month of Ramaḍān, Shawwāl, and Dhū al-Qaʿdah. Then he departed from it on Tuesday, eight nights past from Dhū al-Ḥijjah, the day of al-Tarwiyah, on the day Muslim ibn ʿAqīl departed.

Hārūn ibn Muslim mentioned, from ʿAlī ibn Ṣāliḥ, from ʿĪsā ibn Yazīd, that al-Mukhtār ibn Abī ʿUbayd and ʿAbd Allāh ibn al-Ḥārith ibn Nawfal had departed with Muslim. Al-Mukhtār departed with a green banner, and ʿAbd Allāh departed with a red banner, wearing red clothes. Al-Mukhtār came with his banner and planted it at the door of ʿAmr ibn Ḥurayth, and said: "I have only come out to protect ʿAmr". And Ibn al-Ashʿath, al-Qaʿqāʿ ibn Shūr, and Shabath ibn Ribʿī fought against Muslim and his companions in the evening when Muslim marched to the palace of Ibn Ziyād with intense fighting. And Shabath kept saying: "Wait for them until night, they will disperse." Al-Qaʿqāʿ said to him: "You have blocked the people's way of escape, so let them disperse." And ʿUbayd Allāh ordered that al-Mukhtār and ʿAbd Allāh ibn al-Ḥārith be sought, and he placed a reward for them. They were brought and imprisoned.

Al-Ḥusayn's journey to al-Kūfa

Hishām said, from Abū Mikhnaf: Ṣaqʿab ibn Zuhayr told me, from ʿUmar ibn ʿAbd al-Raḥmān ibn al-Ḥārith ibn Hishām al-Makhzūmī, who said: When the letters from the people of Iraq reached al-Ḥusayn and he prepared to journey to Iraq, I came to him and entered upon him while he was in Mecca. I praised Allah and extolled Him, then said: "To proceed, I have come to you, O son of my uncle, for a matter I wish to mention to you as advice. If you see that you should seek my advice, otherwise I will refrain from saying what I intend to say."

He said: "Speak, for by Allah, I do not think you have a bad opinion, nor is it for an ugly matter or action." I said to him:

> It has reached me that you intend to journey to Iraq, and I am concerned for you about your journey. You are coming to a land where its workers and leaders are, and they have the houses of wealth. The people are slaves to this dirham and dinar, and I do not trust that those who promised you support will fight you, and those who love you more than those who fight you.

Al-Ḥusayn said:

> May Allah reward you well, O son of my uncle, for by Allah, I know that you have walked with advice and spoken with reason, and whatever is decreed will happen, whether I take your opinion or leave it, you are to me the most praiseworthy advisor and the most sincere counselor.

I left him and entered upon al-Ḥārith ibn Khālid ibn al-ʿĀṣ ibn Hishām. He asked me: "Did you meet al-Ḥusayn?" I said to him: "Yes." He said: "What did he say to you, and what did you say to him?" I said to him: "I said such and such, and he said such and such." He said, "By the Lord of the white stone of al-Marwah, indeed, by the Lord of the Sacred House, the best opinion is what you put forth, whether he accepts it or leaves it."

Then he said:

> A seeker of advice
> may deceive and ruin
> And a doubter of the unseen
> may be found sincere.

Abū Mikhnaf related: Al-Ḥārith ibn Kaʿb al-Wālibī told me, from ʿUqbah ibn Samʿān, that when al-Ḥusayn resolved to journey to al-Kūfa, ʿAbd Allāh ibn ʿAbbās ﷺ came to him and said: "O son of my uncle, the people have spread rumors that you are heading to Iraq, so tell me what you are doing?"

He said: "I have resolved to depart on one of these two days, if Allah wills." Ibn ʿAbbās ﷺ said to him:

> I seek refuge with Allah for you from that. Tell me, may Allah have mercy on you! Are you going to a people who have killed their leader, taken control of their land, and expelled their enemy? If they have done that, then go to them. But if they have only invited you while their leader is overpowering them, and his workers are collecting their taxes, then they have only invited you to war and fighting. I do not trust that they will deceive you, lie to you, oppose you, and abandon you, and that they will call upon you, and they will be the most severe people against you."

Al-Ḥusayn ﷺ said to him: "I seek guidance from Allah and will see what happens."

Ibn ʿAbbās ﷺ left him, and Ibn al-Zubayr came to him and talked to him for a while, then said: "I do not know why we have left these people and refrained from them, while we are the sons of the Muhājirīn, and the leaders of this matter without them! Tell me what you intend to do?" Al-Ḥusayn said: "By Allah, I have thought about going to al-Kūfa, and my followers there and the nobles of its people have written to me, and I seek guidance from Allah." Ibn al-Zubayr said to him: "If I had followers like yours there, I would not have chosen anything else." Then he feared that he might be accused, so he said: "If you had stayed in the Ḥijāz and then wanted this matter here, no one would have opposed you, if Allah wills." Then he got up and left him.

Al-Ḥusayn said:

> There is nothing he desires from this world more than for me to leave al-Ḥijāz for Iraq, and he knows that he has no share in my matter, and that the people do not consider him equal to me, so he wishes that I would leave it to be free for him.

When it was evening or the next day, al-Ḥusayn ﷺ came to ʿAbd Allāh ibn ʿAbbās ﷺ who said:

> O son of my uncle, I am patient and not patient. I fear for you in this journey destruction and annihilation. The people of Iraq are treacherous, so do not approach them. Stay in this land, for you are the leader of the people of the Ḥijāz. If the people of Iraq want you as they claim, then write to them to expel their enemy, after which go to them. If you insist on going out, then go to Yemen, for there are fortresses and valleys, and it is a wide and long land, and your father had followers there. You will be isolated from the people, and you can write to the people, send messengers, and spread your call. I hope that what you desire will come to you in safety.

Al-Ḥusayn said to him: "O son of my uncle, by Allah, I know that you are a sincere and compassionate advisor, but I have resolved and decided to depart." Ibn ʿAbbās replied:

> If you are going, then do not take your women and children with you, for by Allah, I fear that you will be killed as ʿUthmān was killed, and his women and children will look at him.

Ibn ʿAbbās continued:

> You have pleased Ibn al-Zubayr by leaving him and the Ḥijāz and because today no one looks at him since you are present. By Allah, who there is no god but Him, if I knew that if I took you by your hair and your forelock until the people gathered around me and you, and you would obey me, I would have done that.

Then Ibn ʿAbbās left him, and passed by ʿAbd Allāh ibn al-Zubayr, and said: "Your eye is pleased, O son of al-Zubayr!" Then he said:

> O you, like a bird in a nest
> The sky is clear for you
> so lay eggs and chirp and peck as you wish.
> This is Ḥusayn going to Iraq
> and you stay in the Ḥijāz.

Abū Mikhnaf related: Abū Janāb Yaḥyā ibn Abī Ḥayyah said, from ʿAdī ibn Ḥurmalah al-Asadī, from ʿAbd Allāh ibn Sulaym and al-Mudrī ibn al-Mushammal al-Asadī, who related:

We went on pilgrimage from al-Kūfa until we arrived in Mecca, and we entered on the day of al-Tarwiyah. We found Ḥusayn and ʿAbd Allāh ibn al-Zubayr standing at the height of the forenoon between the stone and the door. We approached them, and we heard Ibn al-Zubayr saying to Ḥusayn: "If you wish to stay, stay and take charge of this matter, and we will support you, help you, advise you, and pledge allegiance to you." Ḥusayn said to him: "My father told me that there is a ram here that will violate its sanctity, and I do not want to be that ram." Ibn al-Zubayr said to him: "Then stay if you wish and appoint me to the matter, and you will be obeyed and not disobeyed." He said: "I do not want this either." Then they lowered their voices and continued to whisper to each other until we heard the call of the people heading towards Minā at noon. Ḥusayn circumambulated the House and walked between al-Ṣafā and al-Marwah, cut his hair, and ended his ʿUmrah, then headed towards al-Kūfa, and we headed towards the people to Minā.

Abū Mikhnaf related: From Abū Saʿīd ʿAqīṣī, from some of his companions, who said: I heard Ḥusayn ibn ʿAlī while he was in Mecca standing with ʿAbd Allāh ibn al-Zubayr, and Ibn al-Zubayr said to him: "O son of Fāṭimah," and he leaned towards him and whispered to him. Then Ḥusayn turned to us and said: "Do you know what Ibn al-Zubayr is saying?" We said: "We do not know, may Allah make us your ransom!" He said: "He said: 'Stay in this mosque, and I will gather the people for you.'" Then Ḥusayn said: "By Allah, to be killed outside it by a span is more beloved to me than to be killed inside it by a span. By Allah, if I were in the burrow of a snake from these snakes, they would extract me until they fulfill their need. By Allah, they will attack me as the Jews attacked on the Sabbath."

Abū Mikhnaf related: Al-Ḥārith ibn Kaʿb al-Wālibī told me, from ʿUqbah ibn Samʿān who said: When al-Ḥusayn left Mecca, he was intercepted by the messengers of ʿAmr ibn Saʿīd ibn al-ʿĀṣ, led by Yaḥyā ibn Saʿīd. They said to him: "Turn back, where are you going?" He refused and continued, and the two groups pushed each other and fought with whips. Then al-Ḥusayn and his companions resisted strongly, and al-Ḥusayn continued on his way. They called out to him: "O Ḥusayn, do you not fear Allah? You are leaving the community and dividing this nation!" Al-Ḥusayn recited the saying of Allah, the Exalted: "*For me is my work, and for you is your work. You are innocent of what I do, and I am innocent of what you do.*" (Qur'an, 10:41,42)

Then al-Ḥusayn continued until he passed by al-Tanʿīm, where he met a caravan coming from Yemen, sent by Baḥīr ibn Raysān al-Ḥimyarī to Yazīd ibn Muʿāwiyah—who was his governor over Yemen—and the caravan was carrying saffron and garments to be delivered to Yazīd. Al-Ḥusayn captured it and set off with it. Then he said to the camel drivers: "I do not force you, whoever wishes to continue with us to Iraq, we will fulfill their fare and treat them well, and whoever wishes to leave us from this place, we will give them fare according to the distance they have traveled." He said: "Whoever left him was accounted for and their due was fulfilled, and whoever continued with him was given their fare and clothed."

Abū Mikhnaf related, from Abū Janāb, from ʿAdī ibn Ḥurmalah, from ʿAbd Allāh ibn Sulaym and al-Mudrī, who said: We approached until we reached al-Ṣafāḥ, where we met al-Farazdaq ibn Ghālib the poet. He stood before al-Ḥusayn ﵇ and said to him: "May Allah grant you your wish and hope in what you love."

Al-Ḥusayn ﵇ said to him: "Tell us the news of the people behind you." Al-Farazdaq said to him:

> You asked the expert,
> the hearts of the people are with you,
> and their swords are with Banū Umayyah,
> and the decree descends from the sky,
> and Allah does what He wills.

Al-Ḥusayn ﵇ said to him:

> You have spoken the truth, the matter is with Allah, and Allah does what He wills. *Every day our Lord is in a matter.* (Qur'an, 55:29) If the decree comes with what we love, we praise Allah for His blessings, and He is the one who helps in giving thanks. And if the decree prevents hope, then the one whose intention is right and whose inner self is pious will not be disappointed.

Then al-Ḥusayn ﵇ moved his mount and said: "Peace be upon you," and they parted ways.

Hishām said, from ʿAwānah ibn al-Ḥakam, from Lubṭah ibn al-Farazdaq ibn Ghālib, from his father who said: I performed Hajj with my mother, and I was leading her camel when we entered the sanctuary during the days of Hajj, and that was in the year sixty. I met al-Ḥusayn ibn ʿAlī leaving Mecca with his swords and shields. I asked: "Whose caravan is this?" They said: "It belongs to al-Ḥusayn ibn ʿAlī." I went to him and said: "May my father and mother be sacrificed for you, O son of the Messenger of Allah! What made you leave Hajj early?" He said: "If I had not left early, I would have been captured." Then he asked me: "Where are you from?" I said to him: "A man from Iraq." He said: "By Allah," he did not ask me more than that, and he was satisfied with it. He said: "Tell me about the people behind you?" I said to him: "The hearts are with you, and the swords are with Banū Umayyah, and the decree is in the hands of Allah." He said: "You have spoken the truth." He asked me about some matters, and he informed me about vows and rituals. He was heavy-tongued due to a fever he had contracted in Iraq.

Then I continued until I saw a tent pitched in the sanctuary, and it was well-prepared. I went to it and found it belonged to ʿAbd Allāh ibn ʿAmr ibn al-ʿĀṣ. He asked me, and I informed him about meeting al-Ḥusayn ibn ʿAlī. He said to me: "Woe to you! Why didn't you follow him? By Allah, he will rule, and weapons will not be allowed in his presence or among his companions." I intended, by Allah, to join him, and his words affected me. Then I remembered the prophets and their killings, and that prevented me from joining them. I returned to my family in ʿAsfān.

By Allah, I was with them when a caravan arrived from al-Kūfa. When I heard about them, I went after them until I heard their voices and hurried to meet them. I shouted to them: "What happened to al-Ḥusayn ibn ʿAlī?" They replied: "He has been killed." I returned, cursing ʿAbd Allāh ibn ʿAmr ibn al-ʿĀṣ. The people of that time used to say that matter and awaited it every day and night. ʿAbd Allāh ibn ʿAmr used to say: "The tree will not grow, nor the palm tree, nor the small one until this matter appears." I said to him: "What prevents you from selling al-Wahṭ?" He said to me: "May Allah curse so-and-so" — meaning Muʿāwiyah — "and you." I said: "No, rather may Allah curse you." He increased his cursing, and none of his servants were present to stop him. I left, and he did not recognize me — al-Wahṭ is a garden belonging to ʿAbd Allāh ibn ʿAmr in al-Ṭāʾif. Muʿāwiyah had bargained with ʿAbd Allāh ibn ʿAmr for it and offered him a large sum of money, but he refused to sell it for anything.

Al-Ḥusayn continued swiftly, not turning to anything until he reached Dhāt ʿIrq."

Abū Mikhnaf related: Al-Ḥārith ibn Kaʿb al-Wālibī told me, from ʿAlī ibn al-Ḥusayn ibn ʿAlī ibn Abī Ṭālib who said: When we left Mecca, ʿAbd Allāh ibn Jaʿfar ibn Abī Ṭālib wrote to al-Ḥusayn ibn ʿAlī sending it with his two sons: ʿAwn and Muḥammad:

> To proceed, I ask you by Allah to turn back when you read my letter, for I am concerned for you about the path you are taking, that it may lead to your destruction and the extermination of your family. If you perish today, the light of the earth will be extinguished, for you are the guide of the righteous and the hope of the believers. Do not hasten to depart. I am following this letter, and peace be upon you.

ʿAbd Allāh ibn Jaʿfar went to ʿAmr ibn Saʿīd ibn al-ʿĀṣ and spoke to him saying:

> Write to al-Ḥusayn a letter granting him safety, promising him kindness and connection, and assuring him in your letter, asking him to return—perhaps he will be reassured by that and return.

ʿAmr ibn Saʿīd said: "Write what you wish and bring it to me so I can seal it."

ʿAbd Allāh ibn Jaʿfar wrote the letter, then brought it to ʿAmr ibn Saʿīd, who said to him: "Seal it, and send it with your brother Yaḥyā ibn Saʿīd, for he is more likely to reassure him and know that it is serious from you." He did so, and ʿAmr ibn Saʿīd was the governor of Yazīd ibn Muʿāwiyah over Mecca. He said: Yaḥyā and ʿAbd Allāh ibn Jaʿfar caught up with him, then returned after Yaḥyā read the letter to him.

They said: "We read the letter to him and urged him, and he apologized to us by saying: 'I saw a vision in which the Messenger of Allah, peace be upon him, appeared, and I was commanded in it to do something I am proceeding with. 'Alī was more deserving.'" They said to him: "What was that vision?" He said: "I have not told anyone about it, and I will not tell anyone about it until I meet my Lord."

The letter of 'Amr ibn Sa'īd to al-Ḥusayn ibn 'Alī was:

> In the name of Allah, the Most Gracious, the Most Merciful, from 'Amr ibn Sa'īd to al-Ḥusayn ibn 'Alī. To proceed, I ask Allah to turn you away from what will destroy you and guide you to what will benefit you. It has reached me that you have headed towards Iraq, and I seek refuge with Allah for you from discord, for I fear that it will lead to your destruction. I have sent to you 'Abd Allāh ibn Ja'far and Yaḥyā ibn Sa'īd, so come to me with them, for you have safety, kindness, and good neighborliness with me. Allah is my witness and guarantor, and peace be upon you.

He said: Al-Ḥusayn wrote to him:

> To proceed, whoever calls to Allah, the Exalted, and does good deeds and says, 'I am among the Muslims,' does not oppose Allah and His Messenger. You have called to safety, kindness, and connection, but the best safety is Allah's safety, and Allah will not grant safety on the Day of Resurrection to those who do not fear Him in this world. We ask Allah for fear in this world that will grant us safety on the Day of Resurrection. If you intended kindness and connection with your letter, may you be rewarded well in this world and the Hereafter, and peace be upon you.

The narration of 'Ammār al-Duhnī from Abū Ja'far

Zakariyyā ibn Yaḥyā al-Ḍarīr told me, he said: Aḥmad ibn Janāb al-Muṣiṣī told us, he said: Khālid ibn Yazīd ibn 'Abd Allāh al-Qasrī told us, he said: 'Ammār al-Duhnī told us that he said to Abū Ja'far: "Tell me about the killing of al-Ḥusayn as if I were present."

Abū Ja'far related: Ḥusayn ibn 'Alī came with a letter from Muslim ibn 'Aqīl that was sent to him. When he was three miles away from al-Qādisiyyah, he met al-Ḥurr ibn Yazīd al-Tamīmī. He said to him: "Where are you going?" He said: "I am going to this city." He said to him: "Return, for I have not left any good behind me that I hope for." He intended to return, but the brothers of Muslim ibn ʿAqīl who were with him said: "By Allah, we will not return until we take our revenge or be killed." He said: "There is no good in life without you!"

Ḥusayn ibn ʿAlī continued and met the vanguard of ʿUbayd Allāh's cavalry. When he saw that, he turned to Karbalāʾ and backed his position against the reeds so that he would only fight from one direction. He dismounted and set up his tents. His companions were forty-five horsemen and one hundred foot soldiers. ʿUmar ibn Saʿd ibn Abī Waqqāṣ had been appointed by ʿUbayd Allāh ibn Ziyād as the governor of al-Rayy and was given his command.

He said: "Relieve me of this man." He said: "Excuse me." He refused to excuse him. He said: "Give me until the night." He delayed him, and he considered his matter.

When morning came, he went to him, satisfied with what he had been ordered. ʿUmar ibn Saʿd went to al-Ḥusayn. When he came to him, al-Ḥusayn said to him: "Choose one of three options: Either let me return to where I came from, or let me go to Yazīd, or let me go to the frontiers." ʿUmar accepted that, but ʿUbayd Allāh wrote to him: "No, and no honor until he places his hand in my hand!" Al-Ḥusayn said to him: "No, by Allah, that will never happen."

So he fought him, and all of al-Ḥusayn's companions were killed, including several young men from his family. An arrow struck his son who was with him in his lap. He began to wipe the blood from him and said: "O Allah, judge between us and a people who invited us to support us and then killed us."
Then he ordered a cloak to be torn. Then he wore it and went out with his sword. He fought until he was killed. He was killed by a man from Madhḥij who severed his head and took it to ʿUbayd Allāh and said:

> Fill my saddlebags with silver and gold
> For I have killed the veiled king
> I have killed the best of people in terms of mother and father
> And the best of them in lineage

He sent it to Yazīd ibn Muʿāwiyah along with the head. He placed the head before him, and Abū Barzah al-Aslamī was with him. He began to poke at his mouth with a stick and said:

> They split the heads of noble men
> Against us, and they were the most disobedient and oppressive."

Abū Barzah told him: "Raise your stick, for by Allah, I have seen the Messenger of Allah, peace be upon him, kissing his mouth!"

ʿUmar ibn Saʿd sent his women and children to ʿUbayd Allāh, and there was no one left from the family of al-Ḥusayn ibn ʿAlī except a boy who was sick with the women. ʿUbayd Allāh ordered him to be killed, but Zaynab threw herself on him and said: "By Allah, he will not be killed until you kill me!" ʿUbayd Allāh felt compassion for her and left the boy alone. He prepared them and sent them to Yazīd.

When they arrived, Yazīd gathered those who were present from the people of al-Shām, then he brought them in, and they congratulated him on the victory.

A man among them, blue-eyed and red-faced, looked at one of the youthful girls from their daughters and said: "O Commander of the Faithful, give me this one." Zaynab said: "No, by Allah, no honor for you or him unless he leaves the religion of Allah." He repeated it, and Yazīd said to him: "Desist from this."

Then he brought them to his family, prepared them, and sent them to al-Madīnah. When they entered it, a woman from Banū ʿAbd al-Muṭṭalib came out with her hair disheveled, placing her sleeve on her head, meeting them while crying and saying:

> What will you say if the Prophet asks you
> What did you do O the last of the nations!
> With my family and my people after my departure
> Among them are captives and killed, covered in blood
> Was this my reward when I advised you
> That you treat me badly in my kin!"

Al-Ḥusayn ibn Naṣr told me: Abū Rabīʿah told us, he said: Abū ʿAwānah told us, from Ḥuṣayn ibn ʿAbd al-Raḥmān who said: It reached us that Muḥammad ibn ʿAmmār al-Rāzī told us, he said: Saʿīd ibn Sulaymān told us, he said: ʿAbbād ibn al-ʿAwām told us, he said: Ḥuṣayn told us, the people of al-Kūfa wrote to al-Ḥusayn ibn ʿAlī, peace be upon him: "There are one hundred thousand behind you." So he sent Muslim ibn ʿAqīl to them who arrived in al-Kūfa and stayed at the house of Hānī ibn ʿUrwah. The people gathered around him, and Ibn Ziyād was informed of that.

Al-Ḥusayn ibn Naṣr added in his narration: Ibn Ziyād sent to Hānī, who came to him, and he said: "Did I not honor you? Did I not respect you? Did I not do good to you?" He said: "Yes." He said: "What is the reward for that?" Hānī said: "Its reward is that I give you safe conduct." He said: "You give me safe conduct!" He took a stick and struck him with it, and ordered him to be bound, then struck his neck. Muslim ibn ʿAqīl was informed of that, so he went out with many people. Ibn Ziyād was informed of that, so he ordered the palace gates to be closed, and ordered a caller to call: "O cavalry of Allah, mount up," but no one answered him, so he thought he was among a crowd of people.

Ḥuṣayn ibn Abd ar-Raḥmān said: Hilāl ibn Yasāf told me: I met them that night on the road near the Mosque of the Anṣār. They did not pass a road to the right or left without a group of them leaving, thirty or forty, and so on. He said: When they reached the market, and it was a dark night, and they entered the mosque, it was said to Ibn Ziyād: "By Allah, we do not see many people, nor do we hear many voices." He ordered the roof of the mosque to be removed, then ordered torches with fire, and they began to look, and there were about fifty men.

He descended and ascended the pulpit and said to the people: "Separate into groups of four, and each group go to their leader." A group of people rose to fight them, and Muslim was heavily wounded, and some of his companions were killed, and they fled. Muslim went out and entered a house of the houses of Kindah.

A man came to Muḥammad ibn al-Ashʿath while he was sitting with Ibn Ziyād and whispered to him, and he said to him: "Muslim is in the house of so-and-so." Ibn Ziyād said: "What did he say to you?" He said: "Muslim is in the house of so-and-so." Ibn Ziyād said to two men: "Go and bring him to me."

They entered upon him while he was with a woman who had lit a fire for him, and he was washing the blood from himself. They said to him: "Come, the governor calls you." He said: "Make a pact with me." They said: "We do not have the authority to do that."

He went with them until he came to him, and he ordered him to be bound, then said: "Hey, hey, O son of so-and-so" — al-Ḥusayn said in his narration: "O son of so-and-so — you came to take my authority!" Then he ordered him to be struck on the neck.

Ḥuṣayn said: Hilāl ibn Yasāf told me that Ibn Ziyād ordered the area between Wāqiṣah to the road of al-Shām to the road of al-Baṣrah to be taken, and no one was allowed to enter or leave. Al-Ḥusayn marched on, unaware of this, until he met some Bedouins and asked them about the situation, and they said: "By Allah, we do not know, except that we cannot enter or leave al-Kufah."

He continued towards the road of al-Shām towards Yazīd, and the cavalry met him at Karbalā'. He dismounted, invoking Allah and Islam. 'Umar ibn Sa'd, Shimr ibn Dhī al-Jawshan, and Ḥuṣayn ibn Numayr were sent to him.

Al-Ḥusayn invoked Allah and Islam to let him go to the Commander of the Faithful and place his hand in his hand [make the oath of allegiance]. They said: "No, except under the judgment of Ibn Ziyād."

Among those sent to him was al-Ḥurr ibn Yazīd al-Ḥanẓalī, then al-Nahshalī with the cavalry. When he heard what al-Ḥusayn was saying, he said to them: "Will you not accept what these people are offering you! By Allah, if the Turks and the Daylamites asked you for this, it would not be permissible for you to refuse them!"

They refused except under the judgment of Ibn Ziyād. Al-Ḥurr turned his horse's face and went to al-Ḥusayn and his companions. They thought he had come to fight them. When he approached them, he turned his shield and greeted them, then attacked the companions of Ibn Ziyād, fighting them. He killed two of them, then he was killed, may Allah have mercy on him.

It was mentioned that Zuhayr ibn al-Qayn al-Bajalī met al-Ḥusayn while he was performing Hajj, and he joined him. Ibn Abī Baḥriyyah al-Murādī and two other men, ʿAmr ibn al-Ḥajjāj, and Maʿn al-Sulamī went out to him. Ḥuṣayn said: "I saw them."

Ḥuṣayn ibn Abd al-Raḥmān said: Saʿd ibn ʿUbādah told me: Some elders from the people of al-Kūfa were standing on the hill, crying and saying: "O Allah, send down Your victory." I said: "O enemies of Allah, will you not come down and support him!"

He said: Al-Ḥusayn approached, speaking to those sent by Ibn Ziyād. He said: "I saw him wearing a robe of brocade." When he spoke to them, he turned away, and a man from Banū Tamīm named ʿUmar al-Ṭahawī shot an arrow at him. "I saw the arrow between his shoulders, stuck in his robe." When they refused him, he returned to his position.

He said: "I saw them,and they were about one hundred men, including five from the descendants of ʿAlī ibn Abī Ṭālib, sixteen from Banū Hāshim, a man from Banū Sulaym allied with them, a man from Banū Kinānah allied with them, and the son of ʿUmar ibn Ziyād."

Saʿd ibn ʿUbādah told me: "We were soaking in the water with ʿUmar ibn Saʿd when a man came to him and whispered to him, saying: 'Ibn Ziyād has sent Jawāriyah ibn Badr al-Tamīmī to you, and ordered him to strike your neck if you do not fight the people.' He said: 'He jumped to his horse, mounted it, then called for his weapons and wore them. He was on his horse, and he led the people to fight them.'"

Al-Ḥusayn's head was brought to Ibn Ziyād and placed before him. He began to poke at it with his stick, saying: "Abū ʿAbd Allāh had gray hair."

His women, daughters, and family were brought. The best thing he did was to order a place for them in a secluded area, provided them with sustenance, and ordered provisions and clothing for them.

Two boys from them, belonging to ʿAbd Allāh ibn Jaʿfar — or the son of Ibn Jaʿfar — went to a man from Ṭayy and sought refuge with him. He struck their necks and brought their heads, placing them before Ibn Ziyād. He intended to strike his neck and ordered his house to be demolished.

A servant of Muʿāwiyah ibn Abī Sufyān told me [the narrator, Ḥuṣayn ibn Abd al-Raḥmān]: "When Yazīd was brought the head of al-Ḥusayn and placed before him, I saw him crying and saying: 'If there were kinship between Ibn Ziyād and al-Ḥusayn, he would not have done this.'"

Ḥuṣayn ibn ʿAbd al-Raḥmān said: "When al-Ḥusayn was killed, they remained for two or three months, as if the walls were stained with blood at sunrise until the sun ascended in the sky."

Ḥuṣayn ibn ʿAbd al-Raḥmān said: Al-ʿAlāʾ ibn Abī ʿĀthah told me: Ras al-Jālūt (his father) said: "I never passed by Karbalāʾ except that I spurred my mount until I left the place behind." I said: "Why?" He said: "We used to talk about a prophet's child being killed in that place." He said: "I feared that I would be the one. When al-Ḥusayn was killed, we said: 'This is what we used to talk about.' He said: "After that, whenever I passed by that place, I walked and did not spur my mount."

Al-Ḥārith told me: Ibn Saʿd told us, he said: ʿAlī ibn Muḥammad told me from Jaʿfar ibn Sulaymān al-Ḍubʿī, who said: Al-Ḥusayn said: "By Allah, they will not leave me until they extract this heart from inside me. When they do, Allah will send upon them someone who will humiliate them until they become more humiliated than the fragments of the nation." He came to Iraq and was killed at Naynawā on the day of ʿĀshūrāʾ in the year 61.

Al-Ḥārith said: Ibn Saʿd said: Muḥammad ibn ʿUmar told us, he said: Al-Ḥusayn ibn ʿAlī, peace be upon him, was killed in Ṣafar in the year 61, and he was fifty-five years old at that time.

Aflah ibn Saʿīd told me, from Ibn Kaʿb al-Qurẓī, Al-Ḥārith said: Ibn Saʿd told us, he said: Muḥammad ibn ʿUmar told us, from Abū Maʿshar, he said: Al-Ḥusayn was killed ten days into Muḥarram. Al-Wāqidī said: This is more accurate.

Al-Ḥārith said: Ibn Saʿd said: Muḥammad ibn ʿUmar told us, he said: ʿAṭāʾ ibn Muslim told us, from someone who told him, from ʿĀṣim ibn Abī al-Najūd, from Zur ibn Ḥubaysh, he said: The first head raised on a spear was the head of al-Ḥusayn, may Allah be pleased with him and may Allah bless his soul.

Abū Mikhnaf related: From Hishām ibn al-Walīd, from someone who witnessed that, he said: Al-Ḥusayn ibn ʿAlī came with his family from Mecca, and Muḥammad ibn al-Ḥanafiyyah was in al-Madīnah. He said: The news reached him while he was performing ablution in a basin. He said: He cried until I heard his tears falling into the basin.

Abū Mikhnaf related: Yūnus ibn Abī Isḥāq al-Sabīʿī told me, he said: When ʿUbayd Allāh heard of al-Ḥusayn's approach from Mecca to al-Kūfa, he sent al-Ḥuṣayn ibn Tamīm, the chief of his police, who camped at al-Qādisiyyah and organized the cavalry between al-Qādisiyyah and Khafān, and between al-Qādisiyyah and al-Qaṭqaṭānah and to Laʿlaʿ. The people said: "This is al-Ḥusayn heading to Iraq."

Abū Mikhnaf related: Muḥammad ibn Qays told me that al-Ḥusayn approached until he reached al-Ḥājir in the valley of al-Rummah. He sent Qays ibn Mushir al-Ṣaydāwī to the people of al-Kūfa, and he wrote with him to them:

> In the name of Allah, the Most Gracious, the Most Merciful, from al-Ḥusayn ibn ʿAlī to his brothers among the believers and Muslims, peace be upon you. I praise Allah to you, there is no god but Him. To proceed, the letter of Muslim ibn ʿAqīl has reached me, informing me of your good opinion, your unity in supporting us, and your demand for our right. I asked Allah to make our actions good and to reward you greatly for that. I have set out to you from Mecca on Tuesday, eight days into Dhū al-Ḥijjah, the day of al-Tarwiyah. When my messenger arrives, be resolute and diligent, for I am coming to you in these days, if Allah wills. Peace be upon you and the mercy of Allah and His blessings.

Muslim ibn ʿAqīl had written to al-Ḥusayn seventeen nights before he was killed,:

> To proceed, the scout does not lie to his people. The people of al-Kūfa are united with you, so come when you read my letter. Peace be upon you.

Al-Ḥusayn had moved with the children and women with him, not turning aside for anything.

Qays ibn Mushir al-Ṣaydāwī went to al-Kūfa with the letter from al-Ḥusayn. When he reached al-Qādisiyyah, he was captured by al-Ḥuṣayn ibn Tamīm and sent to ʿUbayd Allāh ibn Ziyād. ʿUbayd Allāh said to him: "Go up to the palace and curse the liar, the son of the liar." He went up and said: "O people, this is al-Ḥusayn ibn ʿAlī, the best of Allah's creation, the son of Fāṭimah, the daughter of the Messenger of Allah, and I am his messenger to you. I left him at al-Ḥājir, so respond to him." Then he cursed ʿUbayd Allāh ibn Ziyād and his father, and sought forgiveness for ʿAlī ibn Abī Ṭālib. ʿUbayd Allāh ordered him to be thrown from the top of the palace, and he was thrown, torn apart, and died.

Al-Ḥusayn continued towards al-Kūfa and reached a water source of the Arabs, where he found ʿAbd Allāh ibn Muṭīʿ al-ʿAdawī, who was staying there. When he saw al-Ḥusayn, he stood up to him and said: "May my father and mother be sacrificed for you, O son of the Messenger of Allah! What brings you here?" He assisted him down from his mount. Al-Ḥusayn said to him: "The death of Muʿāwiyah has reached you, and the people of Iraq have written to me, inviting me to them." ʿAbd Allāh ibn Muṭīʿ said to him:

> I remind you of Allah, O son of the Messenger of Allah, let not the sanctity of Islam be violated! I implore you by Allah for the sanctity of the Messenger of Allah, peace be upon him! I implore you by Allah for the sanctity of the Arabs! By Allah, if you seek what is in the hands of Banū Umayyah, they will kill you, and if they kill you, they will not fear anyone after you ever. By Allah, it is the sanctity of Islam that will be violated, and the sanctity of Quraysh and the sanctity of the Arabs, so do not do it, and do not go to al-Kūfa, and do not confront Banū Umayyah.

Al-Ḥusayn refused except to continue, until he reached the water above Zarūd.

Zuhayr ibn al-Qayn Joins al-Ḥusayn ibn ʿAlī

Abū Mikhnaf related: Al-Suddī told me, from a man from Banū Fazārah related: During the time of al-Ḥajjāj ibn Yūsuf, we were in the house of al-Ḥārith ibn Abī Rabīʿah in the Tamārīn, which was given after Zuhayr ibn al-Qayn, from Banū ʿAmr ibn Yashkur from Bajīlah. The people of al-Shām did not enter it, so we were hiding in it. I said to the Fazārī man: "Tell me about when you went with al-Ḥusayn ibn ʿAlī."

The Fazārī man said: We were with Zuhayr ibn al-Qayn al-Bajalī when we came from Mecca, traveling alongside al-Ḥusayn. There was nothing more hateful to us than to travel with him in a place. When al-Ḥusayn traveled, Zuhayr ibn al-Qayn stayed behind, and when al-Ḥusayn stopped, Zuhayr went ahead. Until we stopped that day in a place where we had no choice but to stay with him. Al-Ḥusayn stayed on one side, and we stayed on the other side. While we were sitting and having lunch, a messenger from al-Ḥusayn came and greeted us, then entered and said: "O Zuhayr ibn al-Qayn, Abū ʿAbd Allāh al-Ḥusayn ibn ʿAlī has sent me to you to come to him." He said: Everyone put down what was in their hands as if birds were on our heads.

Abū Mikhnaf related: Dalham bint ʿAmr, the wife of Zuhayr ibn al-Qayn, told me: "I said to Zuhayr: 'The son of the Messenger of Allah sends for you, and you do not go to him! Glory be to Allah! If you went to him and listened to his words! Then you could leave him.' Zuhayr ibn al-Qayn went to him, and it was not long before he came back, rejoicing, with his face beaming He ordered his tent, baggage, and belongings to be brought forward and carried to al-Ḥusayn. Then he said to his wife: "You are divorced, join your family, for I do not want anything but good to come to you because of me."

Zuhayr said to his companions: "Whoever among you wishes to follow me, let them do so, otherwise, this is the last meeting. I will tell you a story: We fought at Balanjar, and Allah granted us victory, and we gained spoils. Salmān al-Bāhilī said to us: "Are you happy with what Allah has granted you and the spoils you have gained!" We said: "Yes." He said to us: "When you meet the youth of the family of Muḥammad, be more joyful in fighting with them than with the spoils you have gained." As for me, I entrust you to Allah.'" Then, by Allah, he remained at the forefront of the people until he was killed.

News of the Killing of Muslim ibn ʿAqīl Reaches al-Ḥusayn

Abū Mikhnaf related: Abū Janāb al-Kalbī told me, from ʿAdī ibn Ḥurmalah al-Asadī, from ʿAbd Allāh ibn Sulaym and al-Mudrī ibn al-Mushammal al-Asadī, who said:

When we completed our pilgrimage, we had no intention except to catch up with al-Ḥusayn on the road to see what would happen to him and his situation. We hurried, our camels trotting quickly, until we caught up with him at Zurūd. When we approached him, we saw a man from al-Kūfa who had turned off the road when he saw al-Ḥusayn.

Al-Ḥusayn stopped as if he wanted him, then left him and continued, and we went towards him. One of us said to his companion: "Let us go to this man and ask him, for if he has news of al-Kūfa, we will know it." We went until we reached him and said: "Peace be upon you." He said: "And upon you be peace and the mercy of Allah." Then we said: "Who is the man?" He said: "An Asadī." We said: "We are Asadīs, who are you?" He said: "I am Bukayr ibn al-Muthāʿibah." We identified ourselves to him, then we said: "Tell us about the people behind you." He said: "Yes, I did not leave al-Kūfa until Muslim ibn ʿAqīl and Hānī ibn ʿUrwah were killed. I saw them being dragged by their feet in the market."

We continued until we caught up with al-Ḥusayn. We traveled with him until he stopped at al-Thaʿlabiyyah in the evening. We came to him when he stopped, greeted him, and he returned our greeting. We said to him: "May Allah have mercy on you, we have news. If you wish, we will tell you openly, and if you wish, secretly." He looked at his companions and said: "There is no secret from such as these."

We said to him: "Did you see the rider who met you last night?" He said: "Yes, I wanted to ask him." We said: "We have verified his news for you and spared you from asking him. He is a man from Asad, one of us, with opinion, honesty, virtue, and reason. He told us that he did not leave al-Kūfa until Muslim ibn ʿAqīl and Hānī ibn ʿUrwah were killed, and he saw them being dragged in the market by their feet."

He said: "Indeed, we belong to Allah, and indeed to Him we will return! May Allah have mercy on them." And he repeated that several times.

We said: "We implore you by Allah for yourself and your family, except that you turn back from this place, for you have no supporter or Shīʿa in al-Kūfa. We fear that they will be against you!" At that moment, the sons of ʿAqīl ibn Abī Ṭālib stood up.

Abū Mikhnaf related: ʿUmar ibn Khālid told me, from Zayd ibn ʿAlī ibn Ḥusayn, and from Dāwūd ibn ʿAlī ibn ʿAbd Allāh ibn ʿAbbās, that the sons of ʿAqīl said: "No, by Allah, we will not leave until we take our revenge or taste what our brother tasted."

Abū Mikhnaf related: From Abū Janāb al-Kalbī, from ʿAdī ibn Ḥurmalah, from ʿAbd Allāh ibn Sulaym and al-Mudrī ibn al-Mushammal al-Asadī, they said: Al-Ḥusayn looked at us and said: "There is no good in life after these men." We knew that he had resolved to continue. We said: "May Allah choose the best for you!" He said: "May Allah have mercy on you both!" One of his companions said to him: "By Allah, you are not like Muslim ibn ʿAqīl, and if you had come to al-Kūfa, the people would have been quicker to you." Then he waited until dawn, and he said to his young men and servants: Increase the water and draw more, then they departed and traveled until they reached Zubālah.

Abū Mikhnaf related: Abū ʿAlī al-Anṣārī told me, from Bakr ibn Muṣʿab al-Muzanī, he said: Al-Ḥusayn did not pass by any people of water except that they followed him until he reached Zubālah. There, the news of the death of his foster brother, ʿAbd Allāh ibn Buqṭar, reached him. He had sent him to Muslim ibn ʿAqīl while on the road, unaware that he had been killed. He was intercepted by the cavalry of al-Ḥuṣayn ibn Tamīm at al-Qādisiyyah and sent to ʿUbayd Allāh ibn Ziyād. Ibn Ziyād said: "Go up to the palace and curse the liar, the son of the liar, then come down so I can decide what to do with you!" He went up, and when he looked over the people, he said: "O people, I am the messenger of al-Ḥusayn, the son of Fāṭimah, the daughter of the Messenger of Allah, to support him and help him against Ibn Marjānah, the son of Sumayyah, the illegitimate."

ʿUbayd Allāh ordered him to be thrown from the top of the palace to the ground, and his bones were broken, but he still had some life in him. A man named ʿAbd al-Malik ibn ʿUmayr al-Lakhmī came and slaughtered him. When he was criticized for that, he said: "I only wanted to relieve him."

Dispersal of the al-Ḥusayn's Iraqi Supporters

Hishām said: Abū Bakr ibn ʿAyyāsh told us, from someone who informed him, he said: By Allah, it was not ʿAbd al-Malik ibn ʿUmayr who came to him and slaughtered him, but a tall, curly-haired man who resembled ʿAbd al-Malik ibn ʿUmayr. That news reached Ḥusayn while he was at Zubālah, so he brought out a letter for the people and read it to them:

> In the name of Allah, the Most Gracious, the Most Merciful. To proceed, we have received terrible news: the killing of Muslim ibn ʿAqīl, Hānī ibn ʿUrwah, and ʿAbd Allāh ibn Buqṭar. Our Shia have abandoned us. Whoever among you wishes to leave, let them leave, there is no blame on them from us.

The people dispersed from him, going right and left, until only those who came with him from al-Madīnah remained with him. He did this because he thought that the Bedouins had followed him, thinking that he was going to a place where the obedience of its people was established for him. He did not want them to travel with him unless they knew what they were heading towards. He knew that if he explained it to them, only those who wanted to support him and die with him would accompany him.

When it was dawn, he ordered his young men to draw water and increase it, then they traveled until they passed by the Batn al-ʿAqabah and stopped there.

Abū Mikhnaf related: Luʾdhān, one of Banū ʿIkrimah, told me that one of his uncles asked al-Ḥusayn, peace be upon him, where he was heading. He told him, after which the man said to him:

> I implore you by Allah to turn back, for by Allah, you will only advance towards spears and the edges of swords. If those who sent for you had spared you the burden of fighting and prepared things for you, and you came to them, that would be a different matter. But in this situation that you describe, I do not think you should do it.

He said to him: "O ʿAbd Allāh, it is not hidden from me, the opinion is as you see, but Allah's will cannot be overcome." Then he departed from there.

Yazīd ibn Muʿāwiyah removed al-Walīd ibn ʿUtbah as governor of Mecca this year and appointed ʿAmr ibn Saʿīd ibn al-ʿĀṣ over it. That was in the month of Ramaḍān. ʿAmr ibn Saʿīd led the people in Hajj that year. Aḥmad ibn Thābit related it from Isḥāq ibn ʿĪsā, from Abū Maʿshar.

Yazīd's governor over Mecca and al-Madīnah this year, after al-Walīd ibn ʿUtbah was removed, was ʿAmr ibn Saʿīd. ʿUbayd Allāh ibn Ziyād was placed over al-Kūfa and al-Baṣrah and their territories. Shurayḥ ibn al-Ḥārith was placed over the judiciary of al-Kūfa. Hishām ibn Hubayrah was placed over the judiciary of al-Baṣrah.

The Killing of al-Ḥusayn, May Allah be Well Pleased with Him

He was killed in Muḥarram on its tenth day, as Aḥmad ibn Thābit told me, who said: A narrator told me, from Isḥāq ibn ʿĪsā, from Abū Maʿshar, and so said al-Wāqidī and Hishām ibn al-Kalbī. We have mentioned the beginning of the matter of al-Ḥusayn in his journey towards Iraq and what happened to him in the year 60, and now we mention what happened to him in the year 61 and how he was killed.

I was told by Hishām, from Abū Mikhnaf, he said: Abū Janāb told me, from ʿAdī ibn Ḥurmalah, from ʿAbd Allāh ibn Sulaym and al-Mudrī ibn al-Mushammal al-Asadī, who said:

Al-Ḥusayn, peace be upon him, continued from Batn al-ʿAqabah until he reached Sharāf. When it was dawn, he ordered his young men to draw water and increase it, then they traveled from there, and they continued their journey until midday.

A man said: "Allāhu Akbar!" Al-Ḥusayn said: "Allāhu Akbar! Why did you say that?" He said: "I saw the palm trees." The Asadīs said to him: "This place has never had palm trees." They said: Al-Ḥusayn said to us: "What do you think he saw?" We said: "We think he saw the tops of the horses." He said: "By Allah, I see that too."

Al-Ḥusayn said: "Do we have a refuge to which we can go, placing it behind us, and facing the people from one direction?" We said to him: "Yes, this is Dhū Ḥusam beside you. Turn to it on your left. If you reach it before the people, it will be as you want." He turned to the left and we turned with him, and it was not long before the tops of the horses appeared to us, so we recognized them, and we returned. When they saw us turning off the road, they turned towards us as if their spears were the stingers of bees, and their banners were like the wings of birds. We raced to Dhū Ḥusam, and we reached it before them.

Al-Ḥusayn ؑ dismounted, and he ordered his tents to be set up. The people came, and they were a thousand horsemen with al-Ḥurr ibn Yazīd al-Tamīmī al-Yarbūʿī until he and his cavalry stood opposite al-Ḥusayn in the heat of the midday, and al-Ḥusayn and his companions were wearing turbans and carrying their swords. Al-Ḥusayn said to his attendants: "Give water to the people and let them drink, and give the horses water to drink." His attendants gave the horses water to drink, and the attendants gave the people water until they were satisfied. They filled the bowls, the pitchers, and the basins with water, then brought them to the horses. When a horse drank three, four, or five times, it was taken away, and another was given water until all the horses were given water.

Hishām said: Laqīṭ told me, from ʿAlī ibn al-Ṭaʿān al-Muḥāribī: I was with al-Ḥurr ibn Yazīd, and I came last among his companions. When al-Ḥusayn saw my thirst and that of my horse, he said: "Kneel the water carrier" - and the water carrier to me is the water skin - then he said: "O son of my brother, kneel the camel," so I knelt it. He said: "Drink, and whenever I drank, the water flowed from the water skin." Al-Ḥusayn said: "Twist the water skin" - meaning bend it. He said: "I did not know how to do it!" He said: Al-Ḥusayn stood up and twisted it, and I drank and gave my horse water.

Al-Ḥurr ibn Yazīd came and traveled to al-Ḥusayn from al-Qādisiyyah, and that was because ʿUbayd Allāh ibn Ziyād, when he heard of al-Ḥusayn's approach, sent al-Ḥuṣayn ibn Tamīm al-Tamīmī - who was in charge of his police - and ordered him to camp at al-Qādisiyyah and place the outposts, organizing what was between al-Qaṭqaṭānah and Khafān. He sent al-Ḥurr ibn Yazīd ahead of him with this thousand from al-Qādisiyyah to meet al-Ḥusayn. He continued to accompany al-Ḥusayn until the time for the noon prayer arrived. Al-Ḥusayn ordered al-Ḥajjāj ibn Masrūq al-Juʿfī to call the *adhān*, and he did. When the *iqāmah* was called, al-Ḥusayn came out in a waist wrapper and a cloak and sandals, praised Allah and extolled Him, then said:

> O people, this is an excuse to Allah, the Exalted, and to you. I did not come to you until your letters came to me, and your messengers came to me, saying: Come to us, for we have no leader, perhaps Allah will unite us with you on guidance. If you are still on that, I have come to you. If you give me what I can be assured of from your pledges and covenants, I will come to your city. If you do not, and you dislike my coming, I will leave you and return to the place I came from.

They were silent and he said to the muezzin: "Establish the prayer." He established the prayer, and al-Ḥusayn ﷺ said to al-Ḥurr: Do you want to lead your companions in prayer? He said: "No, rather you pray and we will pray behind you." Then he entered and his companions gathered around him. Al-Ḥurr returned to his place, entered a tent that had been set up for him, and a group of his companions gathered around him. His companions returned to their ranks, and each man took the reins of his mount and sat in its shade. When it was time for the afternoon prayer, al-Ḥusayn ordered them to prepare for departure. He went out and ordered his caller to call for the afternoon prayer.

He led the people in prayer, then greeted them and turned to face them. He praised Allah and extolled Him, then said:

> To proceed, O people, if you fear Allah and recognize the truth for its people, it will be more pleasing to Allah. We, the Ahl al-Bayt, are more deserving of this authority over you than these claimants who do not have it and who act among you with injustice and aggression. If you dislike us and are ignorant of our right, and your opinion is different from what your letters and messengers brought to me, I will leave you.

Al-Ḥurr ibn Yazīd said to him: "By Allah, we do not know of these letters you mention!" Al-Ḥusayn said: "O ʿUqbah ibn Samʿān, bring out the two saddlebags containing their letters to me." He brought out two saddlebags full of letters and spread them out before them. Al-Ḥurr said: "We are not among those who wrote to you, and we have been ordered not to leave you until we bring you to ʿUbayd Allāh ibn Ziyād." Al-Ḥusayn said to him: "Death is closer to you than that." Then he said to his companions: "Stand up and mount." They mounted and waited until their women had mounted.

He said to his companions: "Let us depart." When they went to depart, the people blocked their way.

Al-Ḥusayn said to al-Ḥurr: May your mother be bereaved of you! What do you want?" He replied:

> By Allah, if anyone other than you from the Arabs had said that to me in the same situation, I would not have refrained from mentioning his mother being bereaved, no matter who he was. But by Allah, I have no way to mention your mother except in the best way I can.

Al-Ḥusayn said to him: "What do you want?" Al-Ḥurr said: "By Allah, I want to take you to ʿUbayd Allāh ibn Ziyād." Al-Ḥusayn said to him: "By Allah, I will not follow you." Al-Ḥurr said to him: "So, by Allah, I will not leave you," and they repeated the statement three times. When the conversation increased between them, Al-Ḥurr said to him:

> I was not ordered to fight you, but I was ordered not to leave you until I bring you to Al-Kūfa. If you refuse, then take a path that does not lead you to Al-Kūfa, nor return you to Al-Madīna. It will be between you and me halfway until I write to Ibn Ziyād, and you write to Yazīd ibn Mu'āwiya if you want to write to him, or to 'Ubayd Allāh ibn Ziyād if you wish. Perhaps Allah will bring about a matter that grants me safety from being afflicted by something from your affair.

He said: "Take this road here and turn away from the road to Al-'Adhīb and Al-Qādisiyya." Between him and Al-'Adhīb was thirty-eight miles. Then Al-Ḥusayn set forth with his companions, and Al-Ḥurr accompanied him.

Abū Mikhnaf related: From ʿUqba ibn Abī al-ʿAyzār, that al-Ḥusayn ﵁ addressed his companions and the companions of al-Ḥurr at al-Bayḍa. He praised Allah and glorified Him, then said:

> O people, the Messenger of Allah ﷺ said: 'Whoever sees a tyrant ruler making permissible what Allah has forbidden, breaking the covenant of Allah, opposing the Sunnah of the Messenger of Allah, and acting among the servants of Allah with sin and aggression,

> and does not change it by action or speech, it is incumbent upon Allah to admit him to the same place (of punishment) as that ruler.' Indeed, these people have adhered to the obedience of Satan, and abandoned the obedience of the Most Merciful, and have manifested corruption, and neglected the limits, and monopolized the spoils, and made permissible what Allah has forbidden, and forbidden what Allah has made permissible. I am more deserving than anyone else to change it. Your letters have reached me, and your messengers have come to me with your pledge of allegiance, that you will not abandon me nor forsake me. If you fulfill your pledge, you will be rightly guided. I am al-Ḥusayn ibn ʿAlī, and the son of Fāṭimah, the daughter of the Messenger of Allah ﷺ. My soul is with your souls, and my family is with your families. You have an example in me. If you do not do so and break your covenant, and remove my pledge from your necks, then by my life, it is not unfamiliar to you. You have done it to my father, my brother, and my cousin Muslim. The deceived is the one who is deceived by you. You have missed your fortune and wasted your share. Whoever breaks his pledge only breaks it against himself, and Allah will suffice you. Peace be upon you and the mercy of Allah and His blessings.

ʿUqba ibn Abī al-ʿAyzār said: al-Ḥusayn stood at Dhū Ḥasm, praised Allah and glorified Him, then said:

> Indeed, the matter has come to what you see, and the world has changed and turned away, and its goodness has gone, and nothing remains of it except a small amount like the dregs of a vessel, and a vile life like a poisonous pasture. Do you not see that the truth is not acted upon, and the falsehood is not refrained from! Let the believer desire to meet Allah rightly. For I do not see death except as martyrdom, and life with the oppressors except as a burden.

Zuhayr ibn al-Qayn al-Bajalī stood up and said to his companions: "Do you speak or shall I speak?" They said: "No, you speak." He praised Allah and glorified Him, then said:

> We have heard your words, may Allah guide you, O son of the Messenger of Allah. By Allah, if the world were to remain for us,

> and we were to be immortal in it, while by helping and supporting you we must abandon it, we prefer to go out with you than staying in it.

Al-Ḥusayn prayed for him and said good things about him, and al-Ḥurr approached him and said: "O Ḥusayn, I remind you of Allah regarding yourself, for I bear witness that if you fight, you will be killed, and if you are fought, you will perish as I see." Al-Ḥusayn said to him:

> Do you threaten me with death! Is there anything more than killing me! I do not know what to say to you! But I say as the brother of al-Aws said to his cousin, and he met him while he wanted to support the Messenger of Allah ﷺ and he said to him: "Where are you going? You are going to be killed," he recited:
>
> I will go, and there is no shame
> in death for a young man
> if he intends the truth
> and strives as a Muslim
> and consoles the righteous men
> with himself
> and leaves a deceived one
> who is deceived and forced.

When al-Ḥurr heard that from him, he withdrew from him, and he was traveling with his companions in one direction and al-Ḥusayn in another direction, until they reached ʿAdhīb al-Hijānāt, where the camels of al-Nuʿmān were grazing. They saw four men coming from al-Kūfa on their mounts, leading a horse for Nāfiʿ ibn Hilāl called al-Kāmil, and their guide was al-Ṭirimmāḥ ibn ʿAdī on his horse, and he was saying:

> O my she-camel,
> do not be frightened by my urging
> and hasten before the dawn breaks
> with the best riders and the best group
> until you reach the noble one
> of noble lineage
> the generous al-Ḥurr, broad-chested

> Allah brought him for a good matter
> and then kept him as long as time lasts.

He said: When they reached al-Ḥusayn, they recited these verses to him, and he said: "By Allah, I hope that what Allah wants for us is good, whether we are killed or victorious." Al-Ḥurr ibn Yazīd approached them and said: "These men from the people of al-Kūfa are not among those who came with you, and I am detaining them or sending them back." Al-Ḥusayn said to him: "I will defend them as I defend myself. These are my supporters and helpers, and you had given me that you would not expose me to anything until a letter comes to you from Ibn Ziyād." He said: "Yes, but they did not come with you." He said: "They are my companions, and they are like those who came with me. Therefore, fulfill what was agreed between me and you, otherwise I will fight you." Al-Ḥurr left them be

Al-Ḥusayn said to them: "Tell us about the people behind you." Mujmaʿ ibn ʿAbd Allāh al-ʿĀʾidhī, one of the four men who came to him, said: "As for the nobles, they have been heavily bribed, their pockets filled, their loyalty bought, and their advice secured. They are united against you. As for the rest of the people, their hearts incline towards you, but their swords will be drawn against you tomorrow." He said: "Tell me, do you know anything about my messenger to you?" They said: "Who is he?" He said: "Qays ibn Mushir al-Ṣaydāwī." They said: "Yes, al-Ḥuṣayn ibn Tamīm captured him and sent him to Ibn Ziyād. Ibn Ziyād ordered him to curse you and your father, but he prayed for you and your father, cursed Ibn Ziyād and his father, called for your support, and informed them of your arrival. Ibn Ziyād ordered him to be thrown from the top of the palace."

Ḥusayn's eyes filled with tears, and he could not hold them back. Then he said: "*Among them are those who have fulfilled their vows, and among them are those who wait, and they have not changed in the least*. (Sūrat al-Mu'minūn, 23:33) O Allah, make Paradise our abode and theirs, and unite us and them in the abode of Your mercy and the rewards of Your stored blessings!"

Abū Mikhnaf related: Jamīl ibn Murthad from Banū Maʿn told me, from al-Ṭirimmāḥ ibn ʿAdī that he approached al-Ḥusayn and said to him:

> By Allah, I see no one with you, and if only these who are with you fight you, they would be enough. Before I left al-Kūfa for you a day ago, I saw the people of al-Kūfa gathered in a way I had never seen before. I asked about them, and it was said: "They have gathered to be inspected and then sent to al-Ḥusayn." I implore you by Allah, if you can avoid advancing towards them even a span, do so! If you wish to settle in a place where Allah will protect you until you see what you decide, and it becomes clear to you what you will do, then travel until I bring you to our mountain, which is called Ajā. We have protected ourselves there from the kings of Ghassān and Ḥimyar, from al-Nuʿmān ibn al-Mundhir, and from the black and the red. By Allah, no humiliation has ever entered upon us. I will travel with you until I bring you to the village, then we will send for the men from Ajā and Salma from Ṭayy. By Allah, it will not be ten days before Ṭayy comes to you, men and riders. Then stay with us as long as you wish. If you are stirred to action, I guarantee you twenty thousand Ṭayy men who will strike with their swords before you. By Allah, no harm will ever reach you while they have a single eye blinking.

Al-Ḥusayn said to him:

> May Allah reward you and your people well! There has been an agreement between us and these people that we cannot turn away from, and we do not know what will happen to us and them in the end!

Al-Ṭirimmāḥ ibn ʿAdī said: I bade him farewell and said to him:

> May Allah protect you from the evil of jinn and humans. I have brought provisions for my family from al-Kūfa, and I have money for them. I will go to them and put it with them, then I will return to you, if Allah wills. If I catch up with you, by Allah, I will be among your supporters.

Al-Ḥusayn said: "If you do so, hurry, may Allah have mercy on you." I knew he was anxious for men, so he asked me to hurry

When I reached my family, I gave them what would suffice them, and I advised them. My family said: "You are doing something with your provisions that you have never done before." I told them what I intended, and I set out on the road of Banū Tha'l until I approached 'Adhīb al-Hijānāt. Samā'ah ibn Badr met me and informed me of al-Ḥusayn's death, so I returned.

He said: al-Ḥusayn continued until he reached the palace of Banū Maqātil and stayed there. He saw a tent pitched.

Abū Mikhnaf related: al-Mujālid ibn Sa'īd told me, from 'Āmir al-Sha'bī, that al-Ḥusayn ibn 'Alī said: "Whose tent is this?" It was said: It belongs to 'Ubayd Allāh ibn al-Ḥurr al-Ju'fī. He said: "Call him to me," and sent for him. When the messenger came to him, he said: "This is al-Ḥusayn ibn 'Alī calling you." 'Ubayd Allāh ibn al-Ḥurr said: "Indeed, we belong to Allah, and indeed to Him we will return! By Allah, I left al-Kūfa only because I did not want al-Ḥusayn to enter it while I was there. By Allah, I do not want to see him or for him to see me." The messenger informed him, and al-Ḥusayn put on his sandals, stood up, and came to him. He greeted him and sat down, then invited him to join him. Ibn al-Ḥurr repeated his statement. Al-Ḥusayn said: "If you do not support us, then fear Allah and do not be among those who fight us. By Allah, no one will hear our call for help and then not support us except that they will perish." He said: "This will never happen, if Allah wills." Then al-Ḥusayn left him and returned to his tent.

Abū Mikhnaf related: 'Abd al-Raḥmān ibn Jundub told me, from 'Uqbah ibn Sam'ān who said: When it was the last part of the night, al-Ḥusayn ordered water to be drawn, then he ordered us to depart, and we did so. When we departed from the palace of Banū Maqātil and traveled for a while, al-Ḥusayn nodded off and then woke up, saying: "*Indeed, we belong to Allah, and indeed to Him we will return,*" and "*praise be to Allah, the Lord of the worlds.*" He did this two or three times. His son 'Alī ibn al-Ḥusayn approached him on his horse and said: "*Indeed, we belong to Allah, and indeed to Him we will return,*" and "*praise be to Allah, the Lord of the worlds.* O my father, may I be your ransom! Why did you praise Allah and seek refuge?" He said: "O my son, I nodded off and saw a rider on a horse who said: 'The people are traveling, and death is moving towards them.' I knew that our souls had been announced to us." He said to him: "O my father, may Allah not show you evil, are we not on the right path? He said:

"Yes, by the One to whom the servants return." He said: "O my father, then we do not care, we die rightly." He said to him: "May Allah reward you with the best reward a child can receive from their parent."

When morning came, he descended and prayed the morning prayer, then hastened to ride. He took to the left with his companions, wanting to separate from Al-Ḥurr's men. Al-Ḥurr ibn Yazīd came to him to stop him and his followers. Whenever he turned them towards al-Kūfa they resisted him and rose up with great force. They continued to travel until they reached Nīnawā, the place where al-Ḥusayn had descended.

A rider on a camel with weapons, carrying a bow, came from al-Kūfa. They all stopped waiting for him. When he reached them, he greeted al-Ḥurr ibn Yazīd and his companions, but did not greet al-Ḥusayn and his companions. He handed al-Ḥurr a letter from ʿUbayd Allāh ibn Ziyād. It read: "To proceed, halt al-Ḥusayn when my letter reaches you, and my messenger arrives. Do not let him settle except in the open, without fortification and without water. I have ordered my messenger to stay with you and not leave you until you carry out my orders. Peace."

When he read the letter, al-Ḥurr said to them:

> This is the letter from the governor ʿUbayd Allāh ibn Ziyād ordering me to halt you in the place where his letter reaches me. This is his messenger, and he has ordered him not to leave me until I carry out his orders.

He looked at the messenger of ʿUbayd Allāh, Yazīd ibn Ziyād ibn al-Muhāṣir Abū al-Shaʿthā' al-Kindī al-Bahdalī and said to him: "Are you Mālik ibn al-Nusayr al-Badī?" He said: "Yes" - he was from Kinda. Yazīd ibn Ziyād said to him: "May your mother be bereaved of you! What have you come for?" He said: "What have I come for! I obeyed my leader and fulfilled my pledge." Abū al-Shaʿthā' said to him: "You disobeyed your Lord and obeyed your leader in your own destruction. You earned disgrace and the fire. Allah Almighty said: '*And We made them leaders inviting to the Fire, and on the Day of Resurrection they will not be helped.*' (Surat al-Qasas, 28:41) Such a one is your leader." Al-Ḥurr ibn Yazīd made the people settle in that place without water and not in a village. They said: "Let us settle in this village," meaning Nīnawā or this village - meaning al-Ghāḍirīyya - or this other one - meaning Shafayyah.

Al-Ḥurr said: "No, by Allah, I cannot do that. This man has been sent to me as a spy." Zuhayr ibn al-Qayn said to him: "O son of the Messenger of Allah, fighting these people is easier than fighting those who will come after them. By my life, those who come after them will be more than we can handle." Al-Ḥusayn said to him: "I will not initiate fighting them." Zuhayr ibn al-Qayn said to him: "Lead us to this village so we can settle there, for it is fortified and on the banks of the Euphrates. If they prevent us, we will fight them. Fighting them is easier for us than fighting those who come after them." Al-Ḥusayn said to him: "Which village is it?" He said: "It is al-ʿAqr." al-Ḥusayn said: "O Allah, I seek refuge with You from al-ʿAqr." Then he halted and that was on Thursday, the second day of Muharram in the year 61.

ʿUmar ibn Saʿd ibn Abī Waqqāṣ Arrives from al-Kūfa

The next day, ʿUmar ibn Saʿd ibn Abī Waqqāṣ arrived from al-Kūfa with four thousand men. The reason for Ibn Saʿd's departure to al-Ḥusayn was that ʿUbayd Allāh ibn Ziyād sent him with four thousand men from al-Kūfa to march to Dastabā. The Daylam had come out to it and taken it over. Ibn Ziyād wrote to him giving him the appointment over al-Rayy and ordered him to set out.

He set up camp with the people at Ḥammām Aʿīn, and when the matter of al-Ḥusayn occurred, he returned to al-Kūfa. Ibn Ziyād called ʿUmar ibn Saʿd and said: "March to al-Ḥusayn, and when we have finished what is between us and him, you will go to your work." ʿUmar ibn Saʿd said to him: "If you see fit to excuse me, may Allah have mercy on you, then do so." ʿUbayd Allāh said to him: "Yes, on the condition that you return our appointment." He said: When he said that to him, ʿUmar ibn Saʿd said: "Give me today to consider."

ʿUmar went to consult his advisors, and none of them advised him except to refrain. Ḥamzah ibn al-Mughīrah ibn Shuʿbah - his nephew - came to him and said: "I implore you by Allah, uncle, not to march against al-Ḥusayn and sin against your Lord and sever your kinship! By Allah, to leave this world and your wealth and the authority of the entire earth if it were yours would be better for you than to meet Allah with the blood of al-Ḥusayn!" ʿUmar ibn Saʿd said to him: "I will do so, if Allah wills."

Hishām said: ʿAwānah ibn al-Ḥakam told me, from ʿAmmār ibn ʿAbd Allāh ibn Yasār al-Juhanī, from his father, he said: I entered upon ʿUmar ibn Saʿd, and he had been ordered to march against al-Ḥusayn. He said to me: "The governor ordered me to march against al-Ḥusayn, and I refused that to him." I said to him: "May Allah guide you, may Allah direct you, do not do it and do not march against him." He said: I left him, and someone came to me and said: "This is ʿUmar ibn Saʿd calling people to march against al-Ḥusayn." I went to him, and he was sitting. When he saw me, he turned his face away, and I knew he had resolved to march against him so I left him.

ʿUmar ibn Saʿd went to Ibn Ziyād and said: "May Allah rectify you! You appointed me to this work, wrote me the appointment, and the people heard of it. If you see fit to carry it out for me, then do so and send to al-Ḥusayn with this army from the nobles of al-Kūfa those who are not less capable or less sufficient in war than me," and he named people to him. Ibn Ziyād said to him: "Do not inform me of the nobles of al-Kūfa, and I do not seek your permission for whom I want to send. Either you march with our army, otherwise return to us our letter of appointment." When he saw that he insisted, he said: "I will march." He marched with four thousand until he descended upon al-Ḥusayn the next day after al-Ḥusayn had descended in Nīnawā.

ʿUmar ibn Saʿd sent ʿAzrah ibn Qays al-Aḥmasī to al-Ḥusayn and said: "Go to him and ask him what brought him and what he wants." ʿAzrah was among those who wrote to al-Ḥusayn and was ashamed to go to him. He requested that of all the leaders who wrote to him, and all of them refused and disliked it. Kathīr ibn ʿAbd Allāh al-Shaʿbī—a brave knight who would not be deterred by anything—stood up and said: "I will go to him, and by Allah, if you wish, I will kill him." ʿUmar ibn Saʿd said to him: "I do not want him killed, but go to him and ask him what brought him."

Kathīr ibn ʿAbd Allāh al-Shaʿbī approached him, and when Abū Thumāmah al-Ṣāʾidī saw him he said to al-Ḥusayn, "May Allah rectify you, Abā ʿAbd Allāh! The worst of the people of the earth and the most daring on blood and the most treacherous have come to you." Abū Thumāmah stood up to him and said: "Put down your sword." He said: "No, by Allah, there is no need for that. I am only a messenger. If you listen to me, I will convey to you what I was sent with, and if you refuse, I will leave you." He said to him: "Then I will hold the hilt of your sword; then speak your need." He said: "No, by Allah, do not touch it." He said to him: "Tell me what you came with, and I will convey it for you, and I will not let you approach him, for you are a wicked person." They cursed each other and Kathīr went back to ʿUmar ibn Saʿd and informed him of the news.

ʿUmar called for Qurrā ibn Qays al-Ḥanẓalī and said to him: "Woe to you, O Qurrā! Go to Ḥusayn and ask him what he came with and what he wants." Qurrā ibn Qays went to him, and when Ḥusayn saw him approaching, he said: "Do you know this man?" Ḥabīb ibn Muẓāhir said: "Yes, this is a man from Ḥanẓalah al-Tamīmī, and he is our nephew. I knew him to have good judgment, and I did not expect him to witness this scene." He came and greeted Ḥusayn and conveyed the message of ʿUmar ibn Saʿd to him.

Ḥusayn said: "The people of your city wrote to me to come, but if they dislike me, I will leave them." Ḥabīb ibn Muẓāhir said to him: "Woe to you, O Qurrā ibn Qays! How can you return to the oppressors! Support this man, by whose ancestors Allah honored you and us with dignity." Qurrā said to him: "I will return to my companion with the answer to his message, and I will consider my opinion." He returned to ʿUmar ibn Saʿd and informed him of the news. ʿUmar ibn Saʿd said to him: "I hope that Allah will spare me from making war and fighting him."

Hishām said, from Abū Mikhnaf, he said: Al-Naḍr ibn Ṣāliḥ ibn Ḥabīb ibn Zuhayr al-ʿAbsī told me, from Ḥassān ibn Fāʾid ibn Bukayr al-ʿAbsī who said: "I testify that the letter of ʿUmar ibn Saʿd came to ʿUbayd Allāh ibn Ziyād while I was with him, and it said:

> In the name of Allah, the Most Gracious, the Most Merciful. To proceed, when I reached Ḥusayn, I sent my messenger to him and asked him what brought him and what he seeks. He said: The people of this land wrote to me, and their messengers came to me, asking me to come, so I did. But if they dislike me, I will leave them."

When the letter was read to Ibn Ziyād, he said:

> Now that our claws have clung to him
> He hopes for escape, but there is no escape!

He wrote to ʿUmar ibn Saʿd:

> In the name of Allah, the Most Gracious, the Most Merciful. To proceed, I have received your letter and understood what you mentioned. Offer Ḥusayn to pledge allegiance to Yazīd ibn Muʿāwiyah, he and all his companions. If he does that, we will consider our opinion. Peace.

When ʿUmar ibn Saʿd received the letter, he said: "I thought that Ibn Ziyād would not accept reconciliation."

ʿUmar ibn Saʿd Prevents al-Ḥusayn from Reaching Water

Abū Mikhnaf related: Sulaymān ibn Abī Rāshid told me, from Ḥumayd ibn Muslim al-Azdī, he said: A letter came from ʿUbayd Allāh ibn Ziyād to ʿUmar ibn Saʿd:

> To proceed, place yourself between Ḥusayn and his companions and the water, and do not let them taste a drop, just as was done to the pious, pure, oppressed Commander of the Faithful, ʿUthmān ibn ʿAffān.

ʿUmar ibn Saʿd sent ʿAmr ibn al-Ḥajjāj with five hundred horsemen, and they descended on the waterway, preventing Ḥusayn and his companions from drinking a drop, and that was three days before the killing of Ḥusayn.

ʿAbd Allāh ibn Abī Ḥuṣayn al-Azdī confronted him - and he was counted among Bajīlah - and said: "O Ḥusayn, do you not see the water as if it were the liver of the sky! By Allah, you will not taste a drop of it until you die of thirst." Ḥusayn said: "O Allah, kill him with thirst, and never forgive him."

Ḥumayd ibn Muslim said: "By Allah, I visited him [ʿAbd Allāh ibn Abī Ḥuṣayn al-Azdī] during his [final] illness, and by Allah, who there is no god but Him, I saw him drinking until he was bloated, then he vomited, then he drank again until he was bloated and could not quench his thirst. He continued like that until he died."

[Abū Mikhnaf] relates: When the thirst became severe for Ḥusayn and his companions, he called his brother, al-ʿAbbās ibn ʿAlī ibn Abī Ṭālib, and sent him with thirty horsemen and twenty foot soldiers, and sent with them twenty water skins. They came until they approached the water at night, led by Nāfiʿ ibn Hilāl al-Jamalī with the banner. ʿAmr ibn al-Ḥajjāj al-Zubaydī said: "Who is the man?" He came and said: "What brings you here?" He said: "We came to drink from this water that you have prevented us from." He said: "Drink and be satisfied." He said: "No, by Allah, I will not drink a drop of it while Ḥusayn is thirsty and those you see among his companions." They attacked him, and he said: "There is no way to give water to these people. We have been placed here to prevent them from water." When his companions approached him, he said to his men: "Fill your water skins."

The foot soldiers rushed and filled their water skins. ʿAmr ibn al-Ḥajjāj and his companions attacked them, and al-ʿAbbās ibn ʿAlī and Nāfiʿ ibn Hilāl repelled them. Then they returned to their camp, and they said: "Proceed," and they stood in front of them. ʿAmr ibn al-Ḥajjāj and his companions attacked them and drove them back a little. Then a man from Ṣadāʾ was stabbed by Nāfiʿ ibn Hilāl, and he thought it was nothing, but it worsened after that, and he died from it. The companions of Ḥusayn brought the water skins and delivered them to him.

ʿUmar ibn Saʿd's Negotiations with Al-Ḥusayn

Abū Mikhnaf related: Abū Janāb told me, from Hānī ibn Thubayt al-Ḥaḍramī - who witnessed the killing of Ḥusayn - who said:

Ḥusayn sent ʿAmr ibn Qurrah ibn Kaʿb al-Anṣārī to ʿUmar ibn Saʿd: "Meet me at night between my camp and your camp." ʿUmar ibn Saʿd went out with about twenty horsemen, and Ḥusayn came with a similar number. When they met, Ḥusayn ordered his companions to withdraw from him, and ʿUmar ibn Saʿd ordered his companions to do the same. We withdrew from them so that we could not hear their voices or their conversation. They spoke for a long time until a portion of the night passed, then each of them returned to their camp with their companions.

People speculated about what was said between them, thinking that Ḥusayn said to ʿUmar ibn Saʿd: "Come with me to Yazīd ibn Muʿāwiyah and leave the two camps." ʿUmar said: "Then my house will be destroyed." He said:

“I will rebuild it for you.” He said: “Then my lands will be taken.” He said: “I will give you better than them from my wealth in al-Ḥijāz.” ʿUmar disliked that. People talked about it and it spread among them without them hearing anything or knowing what actually was spoken.

Abū Mikhnaf related: As for what al-Mujālid ibn Saʿīd, al-Ṣaqʿab ibn Zuhayr al-Azdī, and others among the narrators told us, it is what the group of narrators agreed upon. They said: al-Ḥusayn said: “Choose from me one of three options: Either I return to the place I came from, or I place my hand in the hand of Yazīd ibn Muʿāwiyah and he decides what is between me and him, or you send me to any frontier of the Muslims you wish, and I will be a man among its people, having what they have and bearing what they bear.’“

Abū Mikhnaf related: As for ʿAbd al-Raḥmān ibn Jundub, he told me from ʿUqbah ibn Samʿān, he said:

I accompanied Ḥusayn and traveled with him from al-Madīnah to Mecca, and from Mecca to Iraq, and I did not leave him until he was killed. There was not a word he spoke to the people in al-Madīnah, nor in Mecca, nor on the road, nor in Iraq, nor in the camp until the day of his killing except that I heard it. By Allah, he did not give them what people talk about and claim, that he would place his hand in the hand of Yazīd ibn Muʿāwiyah, nor that they would send him to a frontier of the Muslims. Rather he said: “Leave me to go in this wide land until we see what becomes of the people’s affairs.”

Abū Mikhnaf related: “Al-Mujālid ibn Saʿīd al-Hamdānī and al-Ṣaqʿab ibn Zuhayr told me that they met several times, three or four times, Ḥusayn and ʿUmar ibn Saʿd. He said: ʿUmar ibn Saʿd wrote to ʿUbayd Allāh ibn Ziyād:

> To proceed, Allah has extinguished the fire, united the word, and rectified the affairs of the nation. This is Ḥusayn who has given me assurance that he will return to the place he came from, or that we will send him to any frontier of the Muslims we wish, and he will be a man among the Muslims, having what they have and bearing what they bear, or that he will come to Yazīd, the Commander of the Faithful, and place his hand in his hand, and he will decide

> what is between him and him. In this, there is satisfaction for you and rectification for the nation.'

When ʿUbayd Allāh read the letter, he said: "This is the letter of a man who is sincere to his leader, compassionate to his people. Yes, I have accepted."

Abū Mikhnaf related: Shimir ibn Dhī al-Jawshan stood up and said:

> Do you accept this from him while he has descended in your land next to you! By Allah, if he leaves your land and does not place his hand in your hand, he will be more deserving of strength and honor, and you will be more deserving of weakness and incapacity. Do not give him this position, for it is from weakness. But let him descend under your judgment, he and his companions. If you punish, you are the one who punishes, and if you forgive, that is for you. By Allah, it has reached me that Ḥusayn and ʿUmar ibn Saʿd sit between the two camps and talk most of the night.

Ibn Ziyād said to him: "You have seen well! Your opinion is correct."

Abū Mikhnaf related: Sulaymān ibn Abī Rāshid told me, from Ḥumayd ibn Muslim who said:

Then ʿUbayd Allāh ibn Ziyād called Shimir ibn Dhī al-Jawshan and said to him:

> Take this letter to ʿUmar ibn Saʿd and offer Ḥusayn and his companions to submit to my judgment. If they do, send them to me peacefully, and if they refuse, fight them. If he does, listen to him and obey, and if he refuses, fight them. You are the leader of the people, seize him and strike his neck, and send me his head.

Abū Mikhnaf related: Abū Janāb al-Kalbī told me, then ʿUbayd Allāh ibn Ziyād wrote to ʿUmar ibn Saʿd:

> To proceed, I did not send you to Ḥusayn to refrain from him, nor to negotiate with him, nor to promise him safety and survival, nor to intercede for him with me. See, if Ḥusayn and his companions submit to the judgment and surrender, then send them to me

> peacefully. If they refuse, then advance towards them until you kill them and mutilate them, for they deserve that. If Ḥusayn is killed, trample his chest and back with horses, for he is a disobedient, rebellious, oppressive, and unjust person. It does not matter to me if this harms him after death, but I say that if you kill him, do this to him. If you carry out our order, we will reward you as an obedient listener. If you refuse, then leave our work and our army, and let Shimr ibn Dhī al-Jawshan take over the army, for we have ordered him with our command. Peace be upon you.

Abū Mikhnaf related: From al-Ḥārith ibn Ḥuṣayrah, from ʿAbd Allāh ibn Sharīk al-ʿĀmirī who said: When Shimr ibn Dhī al-Jawshan received the letter, he stood up with ʿAbd Allāh ibn Abī al-Muḥall - whose aunt was Umm al-Banīn, the daughter of Ḥizām, who was with ʿAlī ibn Abī Ṭālib, and she bore him al-ʿAbbās, ʿAbd Allāh, Jaʿfar, and ʿUthmān. ʿAbd Allāh ibn Abī al-Muḥall ibn Ḥizām ibn Khālid ibn Rabīʿah ibn al-Waḥīd ibn Kaʿb ibn ʿĀmir ibn Kilāb said: "May Allah rectify the governor! Our nephews are with Ḥusayn, if you see fit to write them a guarantee of safe-conduct, do so." He said: "Yes, with pleasure." He ordered his scribe to write them a guarantee of safe-conduct, and he sent it with ʿAbd Allāh ibn Abī al-Muḥall with a servant named Kizman. When he arrived, he called them and said: "This is a guarantee of safe-conduct sent by your uncle." The young men said: "Convey our greetings to our uncle and tell him that we have no need for your safe-conduct. Allah's safe-conduct is better than the safe-conduct of Ibn Sumayyah."

Shimr ibn Dhī al-Jawshan Urges ʿUmar ibn Saʿd to Fight al-Ḥusayn

Shimr ibn Dhī al-Jawshan approached with the letter from ʿUbayd Allāh ibn Ziyād to ʿUmar ibn Saʿd. When he arrived and read it, ʿUmar said to him:

> What is wrong with you, woe to you! May Allah not bring your house near, and may Allah curse what you have brought to me! By Allah, I think you are the one who prevented him from accepting what I wrote to him. You have ruined a matter we hoped to fix. By Allah, Ḥusayn will not surrender, for he has a noble soul between his sides.

Shimr said to him: "Tell me, what are you going to do? Will you carry out the governor's order and kill his enemy, or will you leave it to me and the army?" He said: "No, and no honor for you, I will take care of it." Shimr said: "Then go ahead, and you take charge of the men."

He rose to him on Thursday evening, the ninth of Muḥarram. Shimr came and stood before the companions of Ḥusayn and said: "Where are our nephews?" Al-ʿAbbās, Jaʿfar, and ʿUthmān, the sons of ʿAlī ؓ, came out to him and said: "What do you want?" He said: "You, O sons of my sister, are safe." The young men said: "May Allah curse you and your safe-conduct! If you are our uncle, do you grant us safe-conduct while the son of the Messenger of Allah has no safety?"

Then ʿUmar ibn Saʿd called out: "O cavalry of Allah, mount up and rejoice!" He mounted the people and advanced towards them after the afternoon prayer. Ḥusayn was sitting in front of his tent, holding his sword, when he nodded off with his head on his knees. His sister Zaynab heard the noise and approached her brother, saying: "O my brother, do you not hear the sounds approaching?" Ḥusayn raised his head and said: "I saw the Messenger of Allah, peace be upon him, in a dream, and he said to me: 'You will come to us.'" His sister slapped her face and said: "Woe to me!" He said: "There is no woe for you, my sister, be calm, may the Most Merciful have mercy on you!"

Al-ʿAbbās ibn ʿAlī said: "O my brother, the people have come." He rose and said: "O ʿAbbās, ride, may I be your ransom, my brother, and meet them. Ask them what they want and what has changed for them, and inquire about what brought them." Al-ʿAbbās went to them, accompanied by about twenty horsemen, including Zuhayr ibn al-Qayn and Ḥabīb ibn Muẓāhir. Al-ʿAbbās said to them: "What do you want? What has changed for you?" They said: "The governor has ordered us to offer you to submit to his judgment or to fight you." He said: "Do not rush. Let me return to Abū ʿAbd Allāh and present to him what you mentioned." They stopped and said: "Meet him and inform him of that, then we will see what he says."

Al-ʿAbbās returned, galloping to Ḥusayn to inform him of the news. His companions stood, speaking to the people. Ḥabīb ibn Muẓāhir said to Zuhayr ibn al-Qayn: "Speak to the people if you wish, or I will speak to them." Zuhayr said to him: "You started this, so you speak to them." Ḥabīb ibn Muẓāhir said: "By Allah, what a wretched people they are before Allah tomorrow, a people who come to Him having killed the descendants of His Prophet ﷺ and his family, and the worshippers of this city who strive in the early mornings and remember Allah much." ʿAzrah ibn Qays said to him: "You praise yourself as much as you can." Zuhayr said to him: "O ʿAzrah, indeed Allah has purified and guided the soul, so fear Allah, O ʿAzrah, for I am among your sincere advisors. I implore you by Allah, O ʿAzrah, not to be among those who assist the misguided in killing the pure souls!" He said: "O Zuhayr, you were not among us as a supporter of this household, you were an ʿUthmānī." Zuhayr replied:

> Do you not see from my stance that I am among them! By Allah, I have never written to him, nor sent him a messenger, nor promised him my support, but the road brought us together. When I saw him, I remembered the Messenger of Allah ﷺ and his position with him, and I knew what he was facing from his enemy and your party. I decided to support him, to be in his party, and to make myself a shield for him, preserving what you have neglected of Allah's right and the right of His Messenger ﷺ.

Al-ʿAbbās ibn ʿAlī came galloping until he reached them and said:

> O people, Abū ʿAbd Allāh asks you to leave this evening so that he can consider this matter, for this is a matter that has not been discussed between you and him. If we meet in the morning, if Allah wills, we will either agree to what you ask and propose, or we will refuse and return it.

He only wanted to delay them that evening so that he could give his orders and make his will to his family. When al-ʿAbbās ibn ʿAlī conveyed this to them, ʿUmar ibn Saʿd said: "What do you think, O Shimr?" He said: "What do you think, you are the commander, and the opinion is yours." He said: "I wanted not to be." Then he turned to the people and said: "What do you think?" ʿAmr ibn al-Ḥajjāj ibn Salamah al-Zubaydī said: "Glory be to Allah! By Allah, if they were from the Daylamites and asked you for this position, it would be appropriate for you to grant it to them." Qays ibn al-Ashʿath said: "Grant them what they ask, for by my life, they will fight you in the morning." He said: "By Allah, if I knew they would do it, I would not have sent them out this evening."

When al-ʿAbbās ibn ʿAlī came to al-Ḥusayn with what ʿUmar ibn Saʿd had proposed, he said: Return to them, and if you can delay them until the morning and push them away this evening, perhaps we can pray to our Lord tonight, call upon Him, and seek His forgiveness, for He knows that I love prayer for Him, reciting His Book, and abundant supplication and seeking forgiveness!"

Abū Mikhnaf related: Al-Ḥārith ibn Ḥuṣayrah told me, from ʿAbd Allāh ibn Sharīk al-ʿĀmirī, from ʿAlī ibn al-Ḥusayn who said: A messenger came to us from ʿUmar ibn Saʿd and stood where he could hear the voice and said: "We have given you respite until tomorrow. If you surrender, we will send you to our governor, ʿUbayd Allāh ibn Ziyād, and if you refuse, we will not leave you."

Abū Mikhnaf related: ʿAbd Allāh ibn ʿĀṣim al-Fāʾishī told me, from al-Ḍaḥḥāk ibn ʿAbd Allāh al-Mashraqī - a clan from Hamdān - that al-Ḥusayn ibn ʿAlī gathered his companions.

Abū Mikhnaf related: Al-Ḥārith ibn Ḥuṣayrah also told me, from ʿAbd Allāh ibn Sharīk al-ʿĀmirī, from ʿAlī ibn al-Ḥusayn who said: Al-Ḥusayn gathered his companions after ʿUmar ibn Saʿd had returned, and that was near the evening. I approached him to listen, and I was ill. I heard my father saying to his companions:

> I praise Allah, the Blessed and Exalted, with the best praise, and I thank Him in times of ease and hardship. O Allah, I thank You for honoring us with prophethood, teaching us the Qur'an, giving us understanding in religion, granting us hearing, sight, and hearts, and not making us among the polytheists. To proceed, I do not know of companions more loyal or better than my companions, nor a family more righteous and more connected than my family. May Allah reward you all on my behalf. Indeed, I think our day with these enemies will be tomorrow. Indeed, I have given you permission, so go all of you, for you are free from any obligation to me. This night has covered you, so take it as a mount.

Abū Mikhnaf related: ʿAbd Allāh ibn ʿĀṣim al-Fāʾishī - a clan from Hamdān - told me, from al-Ḍaḥḥāk ibn ʿAbd Allāh al-Mashraqī, he said: Mālik ibn al-Naḍr al-Arḥabī and I came to al-Ḥusayn, greeted him, then sat with him. He returned our greeting, welcomed us, and asked us why we had come. We said: "We came to greet you, pray to Allah for your well-being, renew our pledge to you, and inform you of the people's news. We tell you that they have gathered to fight you, so consider your opinion." Al-Ḥusayn said: "Allah is sufficient for me, and He is the best disposer of affairs!" He said: "We felt ashamed and greeted him, and prayed to Allah for him." He said: "What prevents you from supporting me?" Mālik ibn al-Naḍr said: "I have debts and a family, but if you release me from the obligation to stay if I do not find any more fighters, I will fight for you as long as it benefits you and defends you!" He said: "You are released from the obligation." I stayed with him. When night came, al-Ḥusayn ؏ said:

> This night has covered you, so take it as a mount. Then let each man take the hand of a man from my family, and disperse in your lands and cities until Allah grants relief. The people only seek me, and if they capture me, they will be distracted from seeking others.

His brothers, sons, nephews, and the sons of ʿAbd Allāh ibn Jaʿfar said: "We will not do it to remain after you. May Allah never show us that." Al-ʿAbbās ibn ʿAlī began with this statement, and they all spoke similarly.

Al-Ḥusayn Prepares His Men for the Upcoming Battle

Al-Ḥusayn ؏ said:

> O sons of ʿAqīl, it is enough for you to have lost Muslim. Go, for I have given you permission. They said: What will people say! They will say we left our elder, our master, and our cousins, the best of uncles, and did not shoot an arrow with them, did not thrust a spear with them, did not strike a sword with them, and we do not know what they did! By Allah, we will not do it, but we will sacrifice ourselves, our wealth, and our families for you, and we will fight with you until we reach your destination. May Allah curse life after you!

Abū Mikhnaf related: ʿAbd Allāh ibn ʿĀṣim told me, from al-Ḍaḥḥāk ibn ʿAbd Allāh al-Mashraqī, he said: Muslim ibn ʿAwsajah al-Asadī stood up and said:

Will we abandon you without fulfilling our duty to Allah in defending you! By Allah, I will break my spear in their chests, and strike them with my sword as long as its hilt remains in my hand, and I will not leave you. If I have no weapon to fight them with, I will stone them for you until I die with you.

Saʿīd ibn ʿAbd Allāh al-Ḥanafī said:

By Allah, we will not leave you until Allah knows that we have preserved the absence of the Messenger of Allah, peace be upon him, in you. By Allah, if I knew that I would be killed, then brought back to life, then burned alive, then scattered, and that would be done to me seventy times, I would not leave you until I meet my death for you. How can I not do that! It is only one death, then it is the honor that never ends.

Zuhayr ibn al-Qayn said:

By Allah, I wish that I would be killed, then brought back to life, then killed again, until I am killed a thousand times, and that Allah would protect you and these young men from your family from being killed.

A group of his companions spoke with words similar to each other, saying:

By Allah, we will not leave you, but our lives are a sacrifice for you. We will protect you with our necks, foreheads, and hands. If we are killed, we will have fulfilled our duty and completed what is upon us.

Abū Mikhnaf related: Al-Ḥārith ibn Kaʿb and Abū al-Ḍuḥāk told me, from ʿAlī ibn al-Ḥusayn ibn ʿAlī who said: I was sitting in that evening when my father was killed the next morning, and my aunt Zaynab was with me, taking care of me. My father was in his tent with his companions, and with him was Ḥuway, the servant of Abū Dharr al-Ghifārī ؓ, who was repairing his sword. My father was saying:

> O time, fie upon you as a friend
> How many at dawn and at dusk

of a companion or a seeker you have killed
And time is not satisfied with a substitute
The matter is to the Almighty
And every living being will follow the path.

He repeated it two or three times until I understood it, and I knew what he meant. My tears choked me, and I held back my tears and remained silent, knowing that the calamity had descended.

As for my aunt, she heard what she heard, and she was a woman, and women are tender and emotional she could not control herself and rushed, dragging her garment, and she was bareheaded until she reached him. She said: "Oh, my grief! I wish death had deprived me of life! Today, my mother Fāṭimah has died, my father ʿAlī has died, and my brother Ḥasan has died. O successor of the past, and protector of the remaining." Al-Ḥusayn looked at her and said: "O sister, do not let Satan take away your composure." She said: "May my father and mother be sacrificed for you, O Abū ʿAbd Allāh! You have killed yourself for my sake."

He swallowed his grief, and his eyes filled with tears, and he said: "If the sandgrouse were left alone, they would sleep at night." She said: "Woe to me, are you being taken by force? That is more painful to my heart and harder on myself!" She slapped her face, tore her collar, and fell unconscious. Al-Ḥusayn went to her and poured water on her face, and said to her: "O sister, fear Allah and be consoled by Allah's consolation. Know that the people of the earth die, and the people of the heavens do not remain, and everything will perish except the face of Allah, who created the earth by His power and will resurrect the creation, and He is alone. My father is better than me, my mother is better than me, my brother is better than me, and I, they, and every Muslim have an exemplar in the Messenger of Allah."

He consoled her with this and similar words, and said to her: "O sister, I swear to you, fulfill my oath, do not tear your clothes, do not scratch your face, and do not call for woe and destruction upon me if I am killed." He said: Then he brought her and sat her down with me, and he went out to his companions and ordered them to bring their tents closer together, to interlace the ropes, and to be between the tents except for the side from which their enemy would come.

Abū Mikhnaf related: ʿAbd Allāh ibn ʿĀṣim told me, from al-Ḍaḥḥāk ibn ʿAbd Allāh al-Mashraqī who said: When evening came, Ḥusayn and his companions stood the whole night praying, seeking forgiveness, supplicating, and imploring. He said: Their horses passed by us, guarding us, and Ḥusayn was reciting: "*And let not those who disbelieve think that We extend their time for their good. We only extend it for them to increase in sin, and for them is a humiliating punishment. Allah would not leave the believers in the state you are in until He separates the evil from the good.*" (Surah Āli-ʿImrān, 3:178,179) A man from those horses guarding us heard it and said: "By the Lord of the Kaʿbah, we are the good ones, separated from you."

He said: I recognized him and said to Burayr ibn Ḥuḍayr: "Do you know who this is?" He said: "No." I said: "This is Abū Ḥarb al-Sibāʿī ʿAbd Allāh ibn Shahr - he was a joker and a troublemaker, and he was noble, brave, and reckless. Saʿīd ibn Qays sometimes imprisoned him for a crime." Burayr ibn Ḥuḍayr said to him: "O wicked one, does Allah place you among the good ones!" He said to him: "Who are you?" He said: "I am Burayr ibn Ḥuḍayr." He said: "We belong to Allah! It is hard for me! By Allah, I am ruined, I am ruined, O Burayr!" He said: "O Abū Ḥarb, will you not repent to Allah for your great sins! By Allah, we are the good ones, but you are the wicked ones." He said: "I am a witness to that." I said: "Woe to you! Does your knowledge not benefit you!" He said: "May I be your ransom! Who will accompany Yazīd ibn ʿUdhrah al-ʿAnazī from ʿAnaz ibn Wāʾil!" He said: "Here he is with me." He said: "May Allah curse your opinion in any case! You are foolish." Then he left us, and the one guarding us at night among the horses was ʿAzrah ibn Qays al-Aḥmasī, and he was in charge of the horses.

Al-Ḥusayn Arranges His Troops

He said: When ʿUmar ibn Saʿd prayed the morning prayer on Saturday - and it has also reached us that it was on Friday, and that day was the day of ʿĀshūrāʾ - he went out with the people who were with him. He said: Ḥusayn organized his companions, and he prayed the morning prayer with them. He had thirty-two horsemen and forty foot soldiers. He placed Zuhayr ibn al-Qayn on the right wing of his companions, and Ḥabīb ibn Muẓāhir on the left wing of his companions, and he gave his banner to his brother al-ʿAbbās ibn ʿAlī. They placed the tents behind them, and he ordered wood and reeds to be burned behind the tents, fearing that they would come from behind them. Al-Ḥusayn brought reeds and wood to a low place behind them, like a trench, and they dug it in an hour of the night, making it like a trench. Then they threw the wood and reeds into it, and they said: "If they attack us and fight us, we will throw fire into it so that they do not come from behind us, and we will fight the people from one direction." They did so, and it was beneficial for them.

Abū Mikhnaf related: Faḍīl ibn Khudayj al-Kindī told me, from Muḥammad ibn Bishr, from ʿAmr al-Ḥaḍramī who said:

When ʿUmar ibn Saʿd went out with the people, he was in charge of a quarter of the people of al-Madīnah that day, ʿAbd Allāh ibn Zuhayr ibn Sulaym al-Azdī, and in charge of a quarter of Madhḥij and Asad, ʿAbd al-Raḥmān ibn Abī Sabrah al-Juʿfī, and in charge of a quarter of Rabīʿah and Kinda, Qays ibn al-Ashʿath ibn Qays, and in charge of a quarter of Tamīm and Hamdan, al-Ḥurr ibn Yazīd al-Riyāḥī. All of them witnessed the killing of Ḥusayn except al-Ḥurr ibn Yazīd, who joined with Ḥusayn and was killed along with him. ʿUmar placed ʿAmr ibn al-Ḥajjāj al-Zubaydī on his right wing, and Shimr ibn Dhī al-Jawshan ibn Shuraḥbīl ibn al-Aʿwar ibn ʿUmar ibn Muʿāwiyah - who was al-Ḍabbāb ibn Kilāb - on his left wing, and ʿAzrah ibn Qays al-Aḥmasī in charge of the horses, and Shabath ibn Ribʿī al-Riyāḥī in charge of the men, and he gave the banner to Dhūwayd, his servant.

Abū Mikhnaf related: ʿAmr ibn Murrah al-Jamalī told me, from Abū Ṣāliḥ al-Ḥanafī from a servant of ʿAbd al-Raḥmān ibn ʿAbd Rabbih al-Anṣārī who said: I was with my master, and when the people gathered and approached al-Ḥusayn, al-Ḥusayn ordered a tent to be pitched, then he ordered musk to be dissolved in a large basin or dish. Then al-Ḥusayn entered that tent and applied the musk. My master ʿAbd al-Raḥmān ibn ʿAbd Rabbih and Burayr ibn Ḥuḍayr al-Hamdānī were at the door of the tent, their shoulders rubbing against each other, competing to see who would apply the musk after him. Burayr started joking with ʿAbd al-Raḥmān, and ʿAbd al-Raḥmān said to him: "Leave us, by Allah, this is not the time for frivolity." Burayr said to him: "By Allah, my people know that I have never loved frivolity, neither in my youth nor in my old age, but by Allah, I am optimistic about what we are about to face. By Allah, there is nothing between us and the houris except that these people attack us with their swords. I wish they would attack us with their swords." When al-Ḥusayn finished, we entered and applied the musk. Then al-Ḥusayn mounted his steed and called for a Qur'an, which he placed in front of him. His companions fought fiercely in front of him, and when I saw the people had fallen, I escaped and left them.

Abū Mikhnaf related, from some of his companions, from Abū Khālid al-Kāhilī who said: When the horses approached al-Ḥusayn, al-Ḥusayn raised his hands and said:

> O Allah, You are my trust in every distress, and my hope in every hardship. You are my trust and provision in every matter that befalls me. How many worries weaken the heart, diminish the means, betray the friend, and gloat the enemy. I bring it down to You and complain to You, seeking You alone, and You relieve and uncover it. You are the guardian of every blessing, the owner of every good, and the end of every desire.

Abū Mikhnaf related: ʿAbd Allāh ibn ʿĀṣim told me that al-Ḍaḥḥāk al-Mashraqī said: When they approached us and saw the fire blazing in the wood and reeds that we had ignited behind us to prevent them from coming from behind us, a man came to us riding a fully equipped horse. He did not speak to us until he passed by our tents, and he saw that our tents were only wood blazing with fire. He returned and shouted at the top of his voice: "O Ḥusayn, you hastened the fire in this world before the Day of Resurrection!" Ḥusayn said: "Who is this? It seems like Shimr ibn Dhī al-Jawshan!" They said: "Yes, may Allah rectify you! It is him." He said: "O son of the goat herder, you are more deserving to be burned."

Muslim ibn ʿAwsajah said to him: "O son of the Messenger of Allah, may I be your ransom! Shall I not shoot him with an arrow? He is within my reach, and my arrow never misses. The wicked one is among the greatest tyrants." Ḥusayn said to him: "Do not shoot him, for I dislike starting the fight."

Al-Ḥusayn's Final Speech

Ḥusayn had a horse named Lāḥiq, which he mounted his son ʿAlī ibn al-Ḥusayn on. When the people approached him, he returned with his steed and mounted it, then he called out at the top of his voice, a call that most people could hear:

> O people, listen to my words, and do not rush me until I admonish you with what is due to you from me, and until I apologize to you for my coming to you. If you accept my apology and believe my words, and give me justice, you will be happier with that, and you will have no way against me. If you do not accept my apology and do not give justice from yourselves, *"then resolve your affair and your partners, then let not your affair be in doubt for you, then carry it out against me and do not wait."* (Sūrat Yūnus, 10:71) *"Indeed, my protector is Allah, who sent down the Book, and He is the protector of the righteous."* (Sūrat al-Aʿrāf , 7:196)

When his sisters heard his words, they screamed and cried, and his daughters cried, and their voices rose. He sent his brother al-ʿAbbās ibn ʿAlī and his son ʿAlī to them and said to them: "Silence them, for by my life, their crying will increase." When they went to silence them, he said: "May Ibn ʿAbbās not perish." We thought he said this when he heard their crying because Ibn ʿAbbās had told him not to bring them out. When they were silent, he praised Allah and glorified Him, and mentioned Allah with what He is worthy of, and sent prayers on Muḥammad, peace be upon him, and his angels and prophets. He mentioned things that Allah knows and what cannot be counted. By Allah, I have never heard a speaker before or after him more eloquent in speech than him. Then he said:

> To proceed, then trace my lineage and see who I am, then return to yourselves and blame them, and see, is it permissible for you to kill me and violate my sanctity? Am I not the son of the daughter of your Prophet (ṣ)? and the son of his successor and the son of his cousin, and the first of the believers in Allah and the one who confirmed his Messenger with what he brought from his Lord! Is not Ḥamzah the master of martyrs my uncle! Is not Jaʿfar the martyr, the flyer with two wings my uncle! Did it not reach you the widespread saying among you: that the Messenger of Allah (ṣ) said to me and my brother: These two are the masters of the youth of Paradise! If you believe me in what I say - and it is the truth - by Allah, I have never lied since I knew that Allah detests it upon its people, and harms those who fabricate it, and if you disbelieve

> me, then among you are those who, if you ask them about that, will inform you. Ask Jābir ibn ʿAbd al-Anṣārī, or Abū Saʿīd al-Khudrī, or Sahl ibn Saʿd al-Sāʿidī, or Zayd ibn Arqam, or Anas ibn Mālik, they will inform you that they heard this statement from the Messenger of Allah (ṣ) for me and my brother. Is there not in this a barrier for you from shedding my blood!

Shamir ibn Dhī al-Jawshan said to him: "Consider me as one who worships Allah on the edge if I know what you say!" Ḥabīb ibn Muẓāhir said to him: "By Allah, I see you worship Allah on seventy edges, and I testify that you are truthful, you do not comprehend what he says for Allah has sealed your heart."

Then al-Ḥusayn said to them:

> If you are in doubt about this statement, do you doubt the fact that I am the son of the daughter of your Prophet! By Allah, there is no son of the daughter of a Prophet between the east and the west other than me among you or among others, I am the son of the daughter of your Prophet specifically. Tell me, do you seek me for a killed person among you whom I killed, or for wealth of yours that I consumed, or for retaliation for a wound?

They took and did not speak to him. Then he called: "O Shabath ibn Ribʿī and O Ḥijār ibn Abjar and O Qays ibn al-Ashʿath and O Yazīd ibn al-Ḥārith, did you not write to me that the fruits have ripened, the greenery has flourished, and the springs have overflowed, and you are advancing upon a prepared army, so come!" They said to him: "We did not do that," and he said: "Glory be to Allah! Yes, by Allah, you did." Then he said: "O people, if you hate me, then let me turn away from you to my safe place in the land."

Qays ibn al-Ashʿath said to him: "Will you not descend upon the judgment of your cousins, for they will not see you except what you love, and no harm will reach you from them?" Al-Ḥusayn said: "You are the brother of your brother, do you want Banū Hāshim to seek you for more than the blood of Muslim ibn ʿAqīl? No, by Allah, I will not give them my hand like a humiliated person, nor will I acknowledge them like a slave. Servants of Allah, *I have sought refuge with my Lord and your Lord from being stoned.* (Sūrat ad-Dukhān, 44:20) *I seek refuge with my Lord and your Lord from every arrogant person who does not believe in the Day of Judgment.* (Sūrat Ghāfir, 40:26) Then he dismounted his camel, and ordered ʿUqbah ibn Samʿān to tie it, and they advanced towards him.

ʿAlī ibn Ḥanẓalah ibn Asʿad al-Shāmī, narrated to me from a man of his people who witnessed the killing of al-Ḥusayn named Kathīr ibn ʿAbd Allāh al-Shaʿbī who said:

When we advanced towards al-Ḥusayn, Zuhayr ibn Qayn came out to us on a horse with a long mane, armed with weapons, and said:

> O people of al-Kūfah, a warning to you from the punishment of Allah, a warning! It is the duty of a Muslim to advise his fellow Muslim, and we are still brothers, on one religion and one creed, as long as the sword has not fallen between us and you. You are worthy of our advice. But if the sword falls, the protection is cut off, and we become a nation and you become a nation. Allah has tested us and you with the offspring of His Prophet Muḥammad (ṣ) to see what we and you will do. We call you to support them and to abandon the tyrant ʿUbayd Allāh ibn Ziyād, for you will not attain from them except the evil of their entire reign. They will blind your eyes, cut off your hands and feet, mutilate you, hang you on palm trunks, and kill your nobles and reciters, like Ḥujr ibn ʿAdī and his companions, and Hānī ibn ʿUrwah and his likes.

They insulted him, praised ʿUbayd Allāh ibn Ziyād, and prayed for him. They said: "By Allah, we will not leave until we kill your companion and those with him, or we send him and his companions to the governor ʿUbayd Allāh in peace."

Zuhayr said to them:

> Servants of Allah, the children of Fāṭimah, may Allah be pleased with her, are more deserving of love and support than the son of Sumayyah. If you do not support them, I seek refuge with Allah that you kill them. Leave the man and his cousin Yazīd ibn Muʿāwiyah, for by my life, Yazīd will be satisfied with your obedience without killing al-Ḥusayn.

Shamir ibn Dhī al-Jawshan shot an arrow at him and said: "Be silent, may Allah silence your voice, you have wearied us with your many words!" Zuhayr said to him: "O son of the one who urinates on his heels, I am not addressing you! You are but a beast. By Allah, I do not think you know two verses from the Book of Allah. Rejoice in disgrace on the Day of Judgment and painful punishment." Shamir said to him: "By Allah, He will kill you and your companion in an hour." Zuhayr said: "Do you threaten me with death! By Allah, death with him is more beloved to me than eternal life with you."

Then he turned to the people, raising his voice, and said:

> Servants of Allah, do not let this rude and harsh man and his likes deceive you about your religion. By Allah, the intercession of Muḥammad ﷺ will not reach a people who shed the blood of his offspring and his family, and killed those who supported them and defended their sanctity.

A man called out to him and said: "Abū ʿAbd Allāh says to you: 'Come, for by my life, if the believer of the family of Pharaoh advised his people and was eloquent in his supplication, you have advised these people and been eloquent if advice and eloquence were of any benefit!"

Abū Mikhnaf related: From Abū Janāb al-Kalbī, from ʿAdī ibn Ḥurmalah who said: When ʿUmar ibn Saʿd advanced al-Ḥurr ibn Yazīd said to him: "May Allah rectify you! Are you fighting this man?" He said: "By Allah, a fight in which heads will fall and hands will fly." He said: "Do you not accept one of the options he offered you?" ʿUmar ibn Saʿd said: "By Allah, if it were up to me, I would have done it, but your governor has refused that."

Al-Ḥurr ibn Yazīd approached and stood among the people, and with him was a man from his people named Qurrāh ibn Qays. He said: "O Qurrāh, have you watered your horse today?" He said: "No." He said: "Do you want to water it?" He said: "By Allah, I thought he wanted to withdraw and not witness the battle, and he did not want me to see him doing that, fearing I would report him. I said to him: 'I have not watered it, and I am going to water it.' He said: "I left that place where he was. By Allah, if he had told me what he wanted, I would have gone with him to al-Ḥusayn."

Al-Ḥurr ibn Yazīd began to approach al-Ḥusayn little by little. A man from his people named al-Muhājir ibn Aws said to him: "What do you want, O son of Yazīd? Do you want to charge?" He remained silent and was seized by trembling. He said to him: "O son of Yazīd, do you want to charge?" He remained silent and was seized by trembling. He said to him: "O son of Yazīd, by Allah, your matter is suspicious. By Allah, I have never seen you in a position like this. If I were asked who is the bravest man in al-Kūfah, I would not have gone beyond you. What is this that I see from you"! He said: "By Allah, I am choosing between Paradise and Hell, and by Allah, I will not choose anything over Paradise, even if I am cut to pieces and burned." Then he struck his horse and joined al-Ḥusayn. Al-Ḥurr said to him: "May Allah make me your ransom, O son of the Messenger of Allah ﷺ! I am your companion who prevented you from returning, and accompanied you on the road, and brought you to this place. By Allah, who there is no god but Him, I did not think that the people would reject what you offered them, nor that they would reach this position with you. I said to myself: 'I do not mind obeying the people in some of their matters, and they will not see that I have left their obedience.' As for them, they will accept from al-Ḥusayn these options that he offers them. By Allah, if I had thought they would not accept them from you, I would not have done it. I have come to you repentant for what I did, and I am offering myself to you until I die before you. Do you see that as repentance for me?"

He said: "Yes, may Allah accept your repentance and forgive you. What is your name?" He said: "I am al-Ḥurr ibn Yazīd." He said: "You are al-Ḥurr as your mother named you, you are al-Ḥurr, *insha'Allah,* in this world and the hereafter. Dismount." He said: "I am better for you as a horseman than as a foot soldier. I will fight them on my horse for a while and then dismount if that becomes my final decision." Al-Ḥusayn said: "Do what you see fit, may Allah have mercy on you." He advanced before his companions and said: "O people, will you not accept from al-Ḥusayn one of these options he has offered you, so that Allah may spare you from war and fighting?" They said: "This is the commander ʿUmar ibn Saʿd, speak to him." He spoke to him as he had spoken before, and as he had spoken to his companions. ʿUmar said: "I have tried, if I could find a way to do that, I would have done it."

Al-Ḥurr ibn Yazīd said:

> O people of al-Kūfa, may your mothers be bereaved of you and may you weep, for you invited him, and when he came to you, you betrayed him, and claimed that you would fight yourselves for him, then you attacked him to kill him, you held him, and took him by the throat, and surrounded him from all sides, preventing him from traveling in the wide land of Allah until he and his family could be safe. He has become in your hands like a prisoner who cannot benefit himself or repel harm, and you have prevented him, his women, his children, and his companions from the flowing water of the Euphrates, which the Jew, the Magian, and the Christian drink, and the pigs and dogs of the black soil wallow in it, and here they are, struck down by thirst. What a bad legacy you have left for Muḥammad in his offspring! May Allah not give you drink on the day of thirst if you do not repent and turn away from what you are doing today in this hour."

He attacked them with foot soldiers who shot arrows at him, and he advanced until he stood before al-Ḥusayn.

Abū Mikhnaf related, from al-Ṣaqʿab ibn Zuhayr and Sulaymān ibn Abī Rāshid, from Ḥumayd ibn Muslim who said: ʿUmar ibn Saʿd advanced towards them, then called out: "O Dhūwayd, bring your banner closer." He said: He brought it closer, then placed his arrow in the middle of his bow, then shot and said: "Witness that I am the first to shoot."

There was a man among us named ʿAbd Allāh ibn ʿUmayr, from Banū ʿAlīm, who had settled in al-Kūfa and taken a house near the well of al-Jaʿd in Hamdān. He had a wife from Banū al-Namir ibn Qāsiṭ named Umm Wahb bint ʿAbd. He saw the people at al-Nukhaylah preparing to march to al-Ḥusayn. He asked about them, and it was said to him: "They are marching against al-Ḥusayn ibn Fāṭimah, the daughter of the Messenger of Allah, peace be upon him." He said: "By Allah, I have been eager to fight the people of polytheism, and I hope that fighting these people who are attacking the son of the daughter of their Prophet will be easier in reward from Allah than my reward in fighting the polytheists." He entered upon his wife and informed her of what he had heard and what he intended. She said: "You have done well, may Allah guide you to the best of your affairs. Do it and take me with you." He said: He went out with her at night until he came to al-Ḥusayn and stayed with him.

Individual Duels Commence

When ʿUmar ibn Saʿd approached him and shot an arrow, the people began to shoot. When they shot, Yasar, the servant of Ziyād ibn Abī Sufyān, and Sālim, the servant of ʿUbayd Allāh ibn Ziyād, came out and said: "Who will duel? Let some of you come out to us." He said: Ḥabīb ibn Muẓāhir and Burayr ibn Ḥuḍayr jumped up. Al-Ḥusayn said to them: "Sit down." ʿAbd Allāh ibn ʿUmayr al-Kalbī stood up and said: "Abū ʿAbd Allāh, may Allah have mercy on you! Allow me to go out to them." Al-Ḥusayn saw a tall, dark-skinned man with strong arms and broad shoulders. Al-Ḥusayn said: "I think he is a fighter for his peers. Go out if you wish." He went out to them. They said to him: "Who are you?" He identified himself to them. They said: "We do not know you. Let Zuhayr ibn al-Qayn or Ḥabīb ibn Muẓāhir or Burayr ibn Ḥuḍayr come out to us."

Yasar stood in front of Sālim. Al-Kalbī said to him: "O son of the adulteress, you refuse to duel anyone from the people, and no one comes out to you except that they are better than you." Then he attacked him and struck him with his sword until he killed him. He was busy striking him with his sword when Sālim attacked him. He shouted at him: "The servant has overwhelmed you." He said: He did not pay attention to him until he approached him and struck him first. Al-Kalbī blocked it with his left hand, cutting off the fingers of his left hand. Then al-Kalbī leaned on him and struck him until he killed him. Al-Kalbī came forward, chanting while he had killed them both:

> If you don't know me,
> I am the son of Kalb
> My house is in ʿUlaym
> My lineage is strong and firm
> I am not a coward in adversity
> I am committed to you, Umm Wahb
> in attacking them and striking them
> The strike of a young man
> who believes in the Lord.

Um Wahb took a tent-pole, then she approached her husband saying to him: "May my father and mother be sacrificed for you! Fight for the good descendants of Muhammad." He approached her, pushing her towards the women, and she started pulling his garment. Then she said: "I will not leave you until I die with you." Ḥusayn called her and said: "May you be rewarded well from the family, return, may Allah have mercy on you, to the women and sit with them, for there is no fighting for women." So she returned to them.

ʿAmr ibn al-Ḥajjāj attacked, and he was on the right side of the people in the right wing. When he approached Ḥusayn, they knelt on their knees and pointed their spears towards them. Their horses did not advance on the spears, so the horses turned back, and they shot them with arrows, killing some of them and wounding others.

Abū Mikhnaf related: Ḥusayn Abū Jaʿfar related: Then a man from Banū Tamīm named ʿAbd Allāh ibn Ḥawzah came until he stood before Ḥusayn and said: "O Ḥusayn, O Ḥusayn!" Ḥusayn said: "What do you want?" He said: "Rejoice in the fire." Ḥusayn said: "No, I am going to a merciful Lord and an obedient intercessor. Who is this?" His companions said to him: "This is Ibn Ḥawzah." Ḥusayn said: "O Lord, send him to the fire." His horse became agitated in a ditch and he fell into it, his leg got caught in the stirrup, his head hit the ground, and the horse ran away, dragging him and hitting his head against every stone and tree until he died.

Abū Mikhnaf related: As for Suwayd ibn Ḥayyah, he claimed to me that ʿAbd Allāh ibn Ḥawzah when his horse fell, his left leg remained in the stirrup, and his right leg was raised and flew, and his horse ran with him, striking his head against every stone and tree trunk until he died.

Abū Mikhnaf related from ʿAṭāʾ ibn al-Sāʾib, from ʿAbd al-Jabbār ibn Wāʾil al-Ḥaḍramī, from his brother Masrūq ibn Wāʾil who said: I was among the first of the cavalry who went to al-Ḥusayn, and I said: "I will be among the first to reach him, perhaps I will strike the head of al-Ḥusayn and gain a position with ʿUbayd Allāh ibn Ziyād." When we reached al-Ḥusayn, a man from the people named Ibn Ḥawzah came forward and said: "Is al-Ḥusayn among you?" He said: al-Ḥusayn remained silent, and he repeated it a second time, and he remained silent until the third time he said: "Tell him: Yes, this is al-Ḥusayn, what do you want?" He said: "O al-Ḥusayn, rejoice in the fire." He said: "You lied, rather I am going to a forgiving Lord and an obedient intercessor. Who are you?" He said: "Ibn Ḥawzah." He said: al-Ḥusayn raised his hands until we saw the whiteness of his armpits from above his clothes, then he said: "O Allah, send him to the fire."

Ibn Ḥawzah became angry and went to charge at him with his horse, and there was a river between them. His foot got caught in the stirrup, and the horse ran with him, and he fell from it. His foot, leg, and thigh were severed, and the other side of his body remained attached to the stirrup. Masrūq returned and left the horses behind him. I asked him and he said: "I have seen something from the People of the House that I will never fight them again." Then the battle ensued.

Abū Mikhnaf related: Yūsuf ibn Yazīd told me, from ʿAfīf ibn Zuhayr ibn Abī al-Akhnas—who had witnessed the killing of al-Ḥusayn—who said: Yazīd ibn Maʿqil from Banū ʿAmīrah ibn Rabīʿah, an ally of Banū Sulaymah from ʿAbd al-Qays, went out and said: "O Burayr ibn Ḥuḍayr, how do you see what Allah has done to you?" He said: "Allah has done good to me, and Allah has done evil to you." He said: "You lied, and before today you were not a liar. Do you remember when I was walking with you in Banū Lawdhān and you said: ʿUthmān ibn ʿAffān was excessive with himself, and Muʿāwiyah ibn Abī Sufyān was misguided and misleading, and the leader of guidance and truth was ʿAlī ibn Abī Ṭālib?" Burayr said to him: "I testify that this is my opinion and my statement."

Yazīd ibn Maʿqil said to him: "I testify that you are among the misguided." Burayr ibn Ḥuḍayr said to him: "Do you want to duel, and we will call upon Allah to curse the liar and kill the wrongdoer, then come out and I will duel you." They went out and raised their hands to Allah, calling upon Him to curse the liar and kill the wrongdoer. Then each one faced his opponent, and they exchanged two blows. Yazīd ibn Maʿqil struck Burayr ibn Ḥuḍayr a light blow that did not harm him, and Burayr ibn Ḥuḍayr struck him a blow that split his helmet and reached his brain, and he fell as if he had fallen from a height, and Ibn Ḥuḍayr's sword was fixed in his head. It was as if I saw him shaking it from his head. Raḍī ibn Munqidh al-ʿAbdī attacked him and embraced Burayr, and they wrestled for a while. Then Burayr sat on his chest and Raḍī said: "Where are the people of defense and protection?"

Ka'b ibn Jābir ibn 'Amr al-Azdī went to attack him, and I said: "This is Burayr ibn Ḥuḍayr, the reciter who used to teach us the Qur'an in the mosque." He attacked him with a spear and placed it in his back. When he felt the spear, he knelt on him and bit his face, cutting off the tip of his nose. Ka'b ibn Jābir stabbed him until he threw him off, and the spearhead was buried in his back. Then he turned to him and struck him with his sword until he killed him.

'Afīf said: "It was as if I saw the fallen 'Abdī shaking the dust from his cloak and saying: 'You have bestowed a favor upon me, O brother of al-Azd, that I will never forget.'" He said: "I said: Did you see this?" He said: "Yes, I saw it with my own eyes and heard it with my own ears."

When Ka'b ibn Jābir returned, his wife or sister, al-Nawār bint Jābir, said to him: "You helped against the son of Fāṭimah and killed the master of the reciters. You have done a immensely wrong thing, and by Allah, I will never speak to you again."

Ka'b ibn Jābir recited:

> Ask and you will be informed about me while you are reproachful
> On the day of Ḥusayn and the spears are thrusting
> Did I not reach the utmost of what you hated and did not
> On the day of terror, what I am doing is not hidden
> With me is a spear that did not betray its shaft
> And a white sword with two sharp edges
> I drew it among a group whose religion
> Is not my religion, and I am content with the son of Ḥarb
> My eyes have not seen anyone like them in their time
> Nor before them among the people when I was young
> More intense in striking with swords in battle
> Indeed, everyone who defends the sanctuary is a striker
> They endured the thrusts and strikes with patience
> And they fought as if that would benefit them
> Inform 'Ubayd Allāh if you meet him
> That I am obedient to the caliph and listening
> I killed Burayr and then carried the favor
> Of Abū Munqidh when he called: Who will defend?

Abū Mikhnaf related: ʿAbd al-Raḥmān ibn Jundub told me: I heard him during the governorship of Muṣʿab ibn al-Zubayr, saying: "O Lord, we have fulfilled our duty, so do not make us, O Lord, like those who have betrayed." My father said to him: "You are right, and you have fulfilled and honored, but you have brought evil upon yourself." He said: "No, I have not brought evil upon myself, but I have brought good."

They claimed that Raḍī ibn Munqidh al-ʿAbdī responded to Kaʿb ibn Jābir after his statement, saying:

> If my Lord had willed,
> I would not have witnessed their battle
> Nor would Ibn Jābir have bestowed favor upon me
> That day was a disgrace and a shame
> The sons will reproach after the gatherings
> I wish before his killing
> And on the day of Ḥusayn,
> I had been in my grave.

ʿAmr ibn Qurẓah al-Anṣārī went out to fight for Ḥusayn, saying:

> The battalion of the Anṣār knows
> That I will protect the sanctuary
> The strike of a young man
> Not cowardly
> A buyer of Paradise
> For Ḥusayn, my soul and my home.

Abū Mikhnaf related: from Thābit ibn Hubayrah, ʿAmr ibn Qurazah ibn Kaʿb was killed, and he was with al-Ḥusayn, and his brother ʿAlī was with ʿUmar ibn Saʿd. ʿAlī ibn Qurazah called out: "O Ḥusayn, O liar, son of a liar, you misled my brother and deceived him until you killed him." He said: "Allah did not mislead your brother, but He guided your brother and misled you." He said: "May Allah kill me if I do not kill you or die before you." He charged at him, but Nāfiʿ ibn Hilāl al-Murādī intercepted him and stabbed him, knocking him down. His companions carried him and rescued him, and he was treated and recovered.

Abū Mikhnaf related: al-Naḍr ibn Ṣāliḥ Abū Zuhayr al-ʿAbsī told me that when al-Ḥurr ibn Yazīd joined Ḥusayn, a man from Banū Tamīm from Banū Shaqrah, who are Banū al-Ḥārith ibn Tamīm, named Yazīd ibn Sufyān, said: "By Allah, if I had seen al-Ḥurr ibn Yazīd when he went out, I would have followed him with the spear."

While the people were fighting and skirmishing, al-Ḥurr ibn Yazīd charged at the people, reciting the words of ʿAntarah:

> I continued to shoot them
> at the hollow of his throat
> and his chest
> until it was covered in blood.

His horse was struck on its ears and its brow, and his blood was flowing. al-Ḥuṣayn ibn Tamīm - commander of the police of ʿUbayd Allāh whom he sent to al-Ḥusayn, and he was with ʿUmar ibn Saʿd, and ʿUmar appointed him over the heavily armed police, said to Yazīd ibn Sufyān: "This is al-Ḥurr ibn Yazīd whom you wished for." He said: "Yes," and he went out to him and said to him: "Do you want to duel, O al-Ḥurr ibn Yazīd?" He said: "Yes, if you wish," and he went out to him. I heard al-Ḥuṣayn ibn Tamīm say: "By Allah, I will go out to him, as if his soul was in his hand." al-Ḥurr did not delay when he went out to him and killed him.

Hishām ibn Muḥammad said, from Abū Mikhnaf, he said: Yaḥyā ibn Hānī ibn ʿUrwah told me that Nāfiʿ ibn Hilāl was fighting that day, saying:

> I am al-Jamalī
> I am on the religion of ʿAlī.

A man named Muzāḥim ibn Ḥurayth went out to him and said: "I am on the religion of ʿUthmān." He said to him: "You are on the religion of Satan." Then he charged at him and killed him. ʿAmr ibn al-Ḥajjāj shouted to the people: "O fools, do you know who you are fighting! The knights of the city, a determined people, do not let anyone from you face them, for they are few, and they rarely survive. By Allah, if you only threw stones at them, you would kill them." ʿUmar ibn Saʿd said: "You are right, the opinion is what you have seen." He sent to the people, urging them not to let anyone among them duel anyone from them.

Abū Mikhnaf related: al-Ḥusayn ibn ʿUqbah al-Murādī told me, al-Zubaydī said: He heard ʿAmr ibn al-Ḥajjāj when he approached the companions of al-Ḥusayn saying: "O people of al-Kūfa, adhere to your obedience and your unity, and do not doubt the killing of those who have deviated from the religion and opposed the leader." Al-Ḥusayn retorted:

> O ʿAmr ibn al-Ḥajjāj, are you inciting the people against us? Have we deviated, and you have remained steadfast? By Allah, you will know when your souls are taken and you die upon your deeds, who has deviated from the religion and who is more deserving of the fire!

Then ʿAmr ibn al-Ḥajjāj charged at al-Ḥusayn on the right wing of ʿUmar ibn Saʿd from the direction of the Euphrates. They fought for an hour, and Muslim ibn ʿAwsaja al-Asadī, the first of the companions of al-Ḥusayn, was struck down. Then ʿAmr ibn al-Ḥajjāj and his companions withdrew, and the dust settled, and they found him lying there. Al-Ḥusayn walked to him and found him still breathing. He said: "May your Lord have mercy on you, O Muslim ibn ʿAwsaja, *Among them are those who have fulfilled their vow, and among them are those who wait, and they have not changed in the least.*" (Sūrat al-Aḥzāb, 33:23)

Ḥabīb ibn Muẓāhir approached him and said: "It is hard for me to see you fallen, O Muslim. Rejoice in Paradise." Muslim said to him weakly: "May Allah give you good news!" Ḥabīb said to him: "If I knew that I would follow you soon from this hour, I would have loved for you to entrust me with everything that concerns you so that I could fulfill it for you in kinship and religion." Muslim said: "I entrust you with this, may Allah have mercy on you - and he pointed with his hand to al-Ḥusayn - to die for him." Ḥabīb said: "I will do so, by the Lord of the Kaʿbah."

It was not long before he died in their hands. A maid of his cried out and said: "O son of ʿAwsaja! O master!" The companions of ʿAmr ibn al-Ḥajjāj shouted: "We have killed Muslim ibn ʿAwsaja al-Asadī!" Shabath said to some of his companions around him: "May your mothers be bereaved of you! You are only killing yourselves with your own hands, and humiliating yourselves for others. You rejoice that someone like Muslim ibn ʿAwsaja is killed? By the One to whom I have submitted, I have seen him in noble positions among the Muslims! I saw him on the day of the battle of

Azerbaijan — he killed six polytheists before the Muslim cavalry arrived. Is someone like him killed among you, and you rejoice?"

The ones who killed Muslim ibn ʿAwsaja were Muslim ibn ʿAbd Allāh al-Ḍabbābī and ʿAbd al-Raḥmān ibn Abī Khushkārah al-Bajalī. Shimr ibn Dhī al-Jawshan charged at the left wing of the people of the left wing, and they stood firm against him, and they fought him and his companions. He charged at al-Ḥusayn and his companions from all sides. al-Kalbī was killed, having killed two men after the first two, and he fought fiercely. Hānī ibn Thubayt al-Ḥaḍramī and Bukayr ibn Ḥayy al-Taymī from Taym Allāh ibn Thaʿlabah charged at him and killed him. He was the second to be killed among the companions of al-Ḥusayn.

The companions of al-Ḥusayn fought fiercely, and their horses charged, and they were only thirty-two horsemen. They charged at the side of the cavalry of the people of al-Kūfa and scattered them. When ʿAzrah ibn Qays — who was in charge of the cavalry of the people of al-Kūfa — saw that his cavalry was being scattered from all sides, he sent to ʿUmar ibn Saʿd ʿAbd al-Raḥmān ibn Ḥiṣn and said: "Do you not see what my cavalry has been facing since today from this small number! Send men and archers to them." He said to Shabath ibn Ribʿī: "Will you not go to them?" Shabath said: "Glory be to Allah! Do you intend to send the elder of Muḍar and the people of the city in general among the archers! Did you not find anyone else to appoint for this and reward you?"

They continued to see Shabath's reluctance to fight. Abū Zuhayr al-ʿAbsī said: "I heard him during the governorship of Muṣʿab saying: 'May Allah never give the people of this city any good, and may He never guide them to righteousness and not guide them to right conduct. Do you not wonder that we fought with ʿAlī ibn Abī Ṭālib and with his son after him against the family of Abū Sufyān for five years, then we turned against his son, who is the best of the people of the earth, and we fight him with the family of Muʿāwiyah and the son of Sumayyah the adulteress! Misguidance, what misguidance!'"

ʿUmar ibn Saʿd called al-Ḥuṣayn ibn Tamīm and sent with him the heavily armed troops and five hundred archers. They approached al-Ḥusayn and his companions and shot arrows at them. They did not stop until they had hamstrung their horses, and they all became foot soldiers.

Abū Mikhnaf related: Namīr ibn Wāʿilah told me that Ayyūb ibn Musharrah al-Khiyawānī used to say: "By Allah, I hamstrung the horse of al-Ḥurr ibn Yazīd, I shot it with an arrow, and it did not take long before the horse shivered, struggled, and fell." Al-Ḥurr jumped off it like a lion with a sword in his hand, saying:

If you hamstring me,
I am the son of al-Ḥurr
Braver than a lion with a mane.

Ayyūb said: "I have never seen anyone fight like him." The elders of the tribe said to him: "Did you kill him?"He said: "No, by Allah, I did not kill him, but someone else did, and I do not like that I would have killed him." Abū al-Waddāk said to him: "Why?"He said: "They claimed he was one of the righteous. By Allah, if that was a sin, I would rather meet Allah with the sin of wounding and fighting than with the sin of killing one of them." Abū al-Waddāk said to him:

> I do not see you except that you will meet Allah with the sin of killing all of them. Do you see if you shot this one and hamstrung that one, and shot another, and stood in a position, and charged at them, and incited your companions, and increased your companions, and they charged at you, and you hated to flee, and another of your companions did as you did, and another and another, would this one and his companions be killed! You are all partners in their blood.

He said to him: "O Abū al-Waddāk, you make us despair of Allah's mercy. If you were in charge of our reckoning on the Day of Resurrection, may Allah not forgive you if you forgive us!" Abū al-Waddāk replied: "It is as I say to you."

They fought them until midday, the fiercest fight created by Allah, and they could not come to them except from one direction due to the closeness of their tents to each other. He said: When ʿUmar ibn Saʿd saw that, he sent men to demolish their tents from their right and left to surround them.

Three or four of the companions of al-Ḥusayn would slip through the tents, attack the man who was demolishing and looting, kill him, shoot him from close range, and hamstring him. ʿUmar ibn Saʿd ordered them to burn the tents with fire, not to enter a tent or demolish it. They brought fire and began to burn. Al-Ḥusayn said: "Let them burn it, for if they burn it, they will not be able to pass through it to you." And so it was, and they only fought them from one direction.

He said: The wife of al-Kalbī came walking to her husband, sat by his head, wiped the dust from him, and said: "Congratulations on Paradise!" Shimr ibn Dhī al-Jawshan said to a servant named Rustam: "Strike her head with the club." He struck her head and crushed it, and she died on the spot.

Shimr ibn Dhī al-Jawshan charged and stabbed the tent of al-Ḥusayn with his spear, and called out: "Bring the fire so I can burn this tents over its inhabitants!" The women screamed and ran out of the tent. Al-Ḥusayn shouted at him: "O son of Dhī al-Jawshan, you call for fire to burn my house on my family? May Allah burn you with fire!"

Abū Mikhnaf related: Sulaymān ibn Abī Rāshid told me, from Ḥumayd ibn Muslim who said: I said to Shimr ibn Dhī al-Jawshan: "Glory be to Allah! This is not right for you. Do you want to combine two things for yourself — to be punished by Allah's punishment, and to kill children and women? By Allah, killing the men is enough to satisfy you." Shimr said: "Who are you?" I said: "I will not tell you who I am." and I feared, by Allah, that if he knew me, he would harm me before the ruler.

Then a man came to him who was more obedient to him than I was, Shabath ibn Ribʿī, and said: "I have not seen a statement worse than your statement, nor a position more disgraceful than your position. Have you become a terror to women!" I testify that he was ashamed, so he went to leave, and Zuhayr ibn al-Qayn charged at him with ten men from his companions. He attacked Shimr ibn Dhī al-Jawshan and his companions, driving them away from the tents until they retreated. They struck down Abā ʿAzza al-Ḍabbī and killed him. He was one of Shimr's companions. The people gathered around them and outnumbered them. The men of al-Ḥusayn continued to be killed, and when one or two of them were killed, it was noticeable among them, while the attackers were numerous, thus it was not noticeable among them who was killed.

Abū Thumāmah ʿAmr ibn ʿAbd Allāh al-Ṣāʿidī said to al-Ḥusayn ﵇:

> O Abā ʿAbd Allāh, may my soul be sacrificed for you! I see these people have come close to you, and by Allah, you will not be killed until I am killed before you, if Allah wills. I love to meet my Lord after having prayed this prayer, which is now due.

Al-Ḥusayn ﷺ raised his head and said: "You have reminded us of prayer, may Allah make you among those who remember and pray! Yes, this is the first time for the prayer. Ask them to give us respite until we pray." Ḥuṣayn ibn Tamīm said to them: "It will not be accepted." Ḥabīb ibn Muẓāhir said to him: "You claim it will not be accepted! The prayer of the family of the Messenger of Allah, peace be upon him, will not be accepted, and it will be accepted from you, you donkey!" Ḥuṣayn ibn Tamīm charged at them, and Ḥabīb ibn Muẓāhir went out to him, struck his horse's face with his sword, causing it to rear and throw him off. His companions rescued him, and Ḥabīb said: "I swear, if we were equal in number or half of you, you would turn your backs, O worst of people in lineage and ancestry."

He continued to say on that day:

> I am Ḥabīb, and my father is Muẓāhir,
> a knight of battle and war.
> You are more numerous
> and better equipped,
> but we are more faithful
> and patient than you.
> We have a higher argument
> and are more evident in truth,
> more pious and freer from blame than you.

He fought fiercely, and a man from Banū Tamīm attacked him but Ḥabīb hit him on the head with his sword and killed him. He was called Budayl ibn Ṣuraym from Banū ʿAqfān. Another man from Banū Tamīm charged at Ḥabīb and stabbed him, causing him to fall. He tried to get up, but Ḥuṣayn ibn Tamīm struck him on the head with a sword, causing him to fall. The Tamīmī descended and severed his head, and Ḥuṣayn ibn Tamīm said to him: "I am your partner in killing him." The other said: "By Allah, no one killed him but me." Ḥuṣayn ibn Tamīm said: "Give him to me so I can hang him on my horse's neck so that people can see and know that I participated in killing him. Then you can take him and go to ʿUbayd Allāh ibn Ziyād. I have no need for what you are given for killing him." He refused, so his people reconciled between them on this.

He gave him the head of Ḥabīb ibn Muẓāhir, and he paraded it around the camp, hanging it on his horse's neck. Then he gave it back to him. When they returned to al-Kūfa, the other took the head of Ḥabīb and hung it on his horse's chest. Then he went to Ibn Ziyād in the palace. His son al-Qāsim ibn Ḥabīb saw him, and he was a young boy at the time. He followed the horseman, never leaving him. Whenever he entered the palace, he entered with him, and whenever he left, he left with him. The horseman became suspicious of him and said: "What is it with you, my boy, that you follow me!" He said: "Nothing." He said: "Yes, my boy, tell me." He said to him: "This head you have is my father's head. Will you give it to me so I can bury it?" He said: "My boy, the prince will not be pleased if it is buried. I want the prince to reward me well for killing him." The boy said to him: "But Allah will not reward you for that except with the worst reward. By Allah, you have killed someone better than you," and he wept.

The boy waited until he grew up, and he had no ambition except to follow the trace of his father's killer to find an opportunity to kill him to avenge his father. In the time of Muṣʿab ibn al-Zubayr when Muṣʿab invaded Bājumayrā, al-Qāsim ibn Ḥabīb entered Muṣʿab's camp and found his father's killer in his tent. He kept looking for him and seeking an opportunity to catch him off guard. He entered upon him at midday while he was resting and struck him with his sword until he killed him.

Abū Mikhnaf related: Muḥammad ibn Qays told me: When Ḥabīb ibn Muẓāhir was killed, that shook Ḥusayn, and he said at that time: "I count myself and the protectors of my companions." Al-Ḥurr began to recite and say:

> I swear I will not be killed
> Until I kill,
> And I will not be struck today
> Except facing forward.
> I strike them with the sword,
> A decisive strike
> Not retreating from them
> Nor hesitating.

He also recited:

> I strike in their flanks
> With the sword
> For the best of those
> Who settled in Minā
> And al-Khayf.

He and Zuhayr ibn al-Qayn fought fiercely. When one of them charged, if he was overwhelmed, the other would charge to rescue him. They did this for a while. Then the foot soldiers attacked al-Ḥurr ibn Yazīd and killed him. Abū Thumāmah al-Ṣāʿidī killed his cousin, who was his enemy.

Then they prayed the noon prayer. Al-Ḥusayn led them in the prayer of fear. Then they fought again after the noon prayer, and their fighting intensified. They reached al-Ḥusayn, and al-Ḥanafī stepped forward in front of him, standing as a target for them, being shot with arrows from the right and left, standing right in front of al-Ḥusayn. He continued to be shot until he fell. Zuhayr ibn al-Qayn fought fiercely and said:

> I am Zuhayr
> and I am the son of al-Qayn
> I defend them with the sword
> for Ḥusayn.

And he began to strike on the shoulder of Ḥusayn and say: "Advance, guided and rightly guided one, for today you will meet your grandfather, the Prophet, and Ḥasan, and the chosen one, ʿAlī, and the one with two wings, the noble young man, and the lion of Allah, the living martyr." Then Kathīr ibn ʿAbd Allāh al-Shaʿbī and Muhājir ibn Aws attacked Zuhayr ibn al-Qayn and killed him.

Nāfiʿ ibn Hilāl al-Jamalī had written his name on the fletchings of his arrows, and he began to shoot them, marked, while saying:

> I am al-Jamalī,
> I am on the religion of ʿAlī.

He killed twelve of the companions of ʿUmar ibn Saʿd besides those he wounded. He fought until his arms were broken and he was captured. Shimr ibn Dhī al-Jawshan took him with his companions, driving Nāfiʿ until they brought him to ʿUmar ibn Saʿd. ʿUmar ibn Saʿd said to him: "Woe to you, O Nāfiʿ! What drove you to do what you did to yourself!" He said: "My Lord knows what I intended." and the blood was flowing down his beard, and he continued: "By Allah, I have killed twelve of you besides those I wounded, and I do not blame myself for the effort, and if I had an arm and a hand left, you would not have captured me." Shimr said to him: "Kill him, may Allah rectify you!" He said: "You brought him, so if you wish, kill him." Shimr drew his sword and Nāfiʿ said to him: "By Allah, if you were among the Muslims, how immense it would be for you to meet Allah with our blood on your hands. Praise be to Allah who made our deaths at the hands of the worst of His creation." Then Shimr killed him.

Then Shimr advanced, attacking them while saying:

> Leave the enemies of Allah,
> Leave Shimr,
> He strikes them with his sword
> And does not flee
> He is for you a poison
> And a deadly enemy.

The Companions of al-Ḥusayn Defend His Person

When the companions of al-Ḥusayn saw that the enemy had become numerous, and they could not protect Ḥusayn or themselves, they competed to be killed in front of him. ʿAbd Allāh and ʿAbd al-Raḥmān, the sons of ʿAzrah al-Ghifārī, came to him and said: "O Abā ʿAbd Allāh, peace be upon you. The enemy has driven us to you, and we wish to be killed before you, to protect you and defend you." He said: "Welcome! Come closer to me." They came closer to him and began to fight near him, and one of them said:

> Indeed, Banū Ghifār and Khindif
> After Banū Nizār know truly
> That we will strike the wicked
> With every sharp and cutting sword.
> O people, defend the noble ones

With the sharp sword
And the piercing spear.

He said: The two young men from Banū Jābir, Sayf ibn al-Ḥārith ibn Surayʿ and Mālik ibn ʿAbd ibn Surayʿ, who were cousins and brothers from their mother, came to Ḥusayn and approached him while they were crying. He said: "O sons of my brother, why are you crying? By Allah, I hope that you will be at peace in an hour." They said: "May Allah make us your ransom! By Allah, we are not crying for ourselves, but we are crying for you. We see that you are surrounded, and we cannot protect you." He said: "May Allah reward you, O sons of my brother, for your unity and your support for me with yourselves, the best reward for the righteous."

Ḥanẓalah ibn Asʿad al-Shabāmī came and stood before Ḥusayn and began to call out:

> O people, I fear for you the like of the day of the confederates. The like of the fate of the people of Nūḥ and ʿĀd and Thamūd and those after them, and Allah does not wish injustice for His servants. O people, I fear for you the day of calling, the day you will turn back fleeing, you will have no protector from Allah, and whoever Allah misguides, there is no guide for them. O people, do not kill Ḥusayn, lest Allah destroy you with punishment, and indeed, the one who fabricates has failed.

Ḥusayn said to him: "O son of Asʿad, may Allah have mercy on you, they have deserved the punishment when they rejected what you called them to of the truth, and they rose against you to violate you and your companions. How are they now that they have killed your righteous brothers!"

He said: "You are right, may I be your ransom! You are more knowledgeable than me and more deserving of that. Shall we go to the hereafter and join our brothers?" He said: "Go to what is better than this world and all that is in it, and to a kingdom that does not perish." He said: "Peace be upon you, Abā ʿAbd Allāh. Peace be upon you and your family, and may Allah unite us with you in His Paradise. He said: Amen, Amen."

Ḥanẓalah advanced and fought until he was killed. Then the two young men from Banū Jābir approached, turning to Ḥusayn and saying: "Peace be upon you, O son of the Messenger of Allah." He said: "And peace be upon you both, and the mercy of Allah." They fought until they were killed.

Then ʿĀbis ibn Abī Shabīb al-Shākirī came with Shawdhub, the servant of Shākir, and said: "O Shawdhub, what do you intend to do?" He said: "What can I do! I will fight with you for the son of the daughter of the Messenger of Allah, peace be upon him, until I am killed." He said:

> That is what I expect from you. If not, then advance before Abā ʿAbd Allāh so that he may count you among his companions, and I may count you as well. If I had anyone with me now, I would prefer them to advance before me so that I may count them. This is a day when we should seek reward with everything we can, for there is no action after today, only reckoning.

He advanced and greeted al-Ḥusayn, then went and fought until he was killed.

Then ʿĀbis ibn Abī Shabīb said:

> O Abā ʿAbd Allāh, by Allah, there is no one on the face of the earth, near or far, more dear to me or more beloved to me than you. If I could protect you from harm and death with something more precious to me than my own life and blood, I would do it. Peace be upon you, O Abā ʿAbd Allāh. I testify to Allah that I am on your guidance and the guidance of your father.

Then he walked with his sword drawn towards them, with a wound on his forehead.

Abū Mikhnaf relates: Namīr ibn Wāʾilah told me, from a man from Banū ʿAbd from Hamdān named Rabīʿ ibn Tamīm, who witnessed that day, who said:

When I saw him approaching, I recognized him, for I had seen him in battles, and he was the bravest of people. I said: "'O people, this is the black lion, this is the son of Abī Shabīb, do not let anyone go out to him." He began to call out: "Is there no man for a man!" ʿUmar ibn Saʿd said: "Stone him with stones." He was pelted with stones from all sides. When he saw that, he threw off his armor and helmet, then charged at the people. By Allah, I saw him driving back more than two hundred people. Then they surrounded him from all sides and killed him. I saw his head in the hands of several men, one saying: "I killed him," and another saying: "I killed him." They went to ʿUmar ibn Saʿd and said: "Do not argue, this man was not killed by one spear." He separated them with this statement.

Abū Mikhnaf related: ʿAbd Allāh ibn ʿĀṣim told me, from al-Ḍaḥḥāk ibn ʿAbd Allāh al-Mashraqī who said: When I saw the companions of al-Ḥusayn had been struck, and it had reached him and his family, and no one remained with him except Suwayd ibn ʿAmr ibn Abī al-Muṭāʿ al-Khathʿamī and Bashīr ibn ʿAmr al-Ḥaḍramī, I said to him: 'O son of the Messenger of Allah, you know what was between you and me. I said to you: I will fight for you as long as I see fighters, and if I do not see fighters, I am free to leave.' He said to me: 'Yes. You have spoken the truth, and how will you find refuge! If you can do that, you are free to leave.'"

I went to my horse, and when I saw the horses of our companions being hamstrung. I brought it and entered it into a tent of our companions among the houses, and I fought with them on foot. I killed two men that day in front of al-Ḥusayn, and I cut off the hand of another. Al-Ḥusayn said to me several times that day: "May your hand not be paralyzed, may Allah not cut off your hand, may Allah reward you well on behalf of the family of your Prophet!"

When he gave me permission, I brought out the horse from the tent, mounted it, and struck it until it stood on its hooves. I rode it across the people, and they made way for me. Fifteen men followed me until I reached Shafiyyah, a village near the Euphrates. When they caught up with me, I turned on them. Kathīr ibn ʿAbd Allāh al-Shaʿbī, Ayyūb ibn Musharrah al-Khiyawānī, and Qays ibn ʿAbd Allāh al-Ṣāʿidī recognized me and said: 'This is al-Ḍaḥḥāk ibn ʿAbd Allāh al-Mashraqī, this is our cousin. We implore you by Allah to leave him alone!' Three men from Banū Tamīm who were with them said: 'By Allah, we will respond to our brothers and the people of our call to what they love by leaving their companion alone.'" When the Tamīmīs supported my companions, the others stopped. He said: "Allah saved me."

Abū Mikhnaf related: Faḍīl ibn Khudayj al-Kindī told me that Yazīd ibn Ziyād, who was Abū al-Shaʿthāʾ al-Kindī from Banū Bahdalah, knelt on his knees in front of al-Ḥusayn and shot a hundred arrows, of which only five missed. He was an archer, and every time he shot, he said: "I am the son of Bahdalah, the knights of al-ʿArjalah. Al-Ḥusayn said: "O Allah, guide his aim, and make his reward Paradise." When he shot, he stood up and said: "Only five arrows missed, and I have killed five men." He was among the first to be killed, and his battle cry that day was:

> I am Yazīd, and my father is Muhāṣir,
> braver than a lion in its den.
> O Lord, I am a supporter of al-Ḥusayn
> and a deserter of Ibn Saʿd.

Yazīd ibn Ziyād ibn Muhāṣir was among those who went out with ʿUmar ibn Saʿd to al-Ḥusayn. When they rejected the conditions of al-Ḥusayn, he turned to them and fought with him until he was killed. As for al-Ṣaydāwī ʿUmar ibn Khālid, Jābir ibn al-Ḥārith al-Salmānī, Saʿd, the servant of ʿUmar ibn Khālid, and Mujmaʿ ibn ʿAbd Allāh al-ʿĀʾidhī, they fought in the first battle. They charged forward with their swords against the people. When they penetrated deeply, the people turned on them and began to push them back, cutting them off from their companions not far away. Al-ʿAbbās ibn ʿAlī charged at them and rescued them. They came back wounded. When their enemies approached them, they charged with their swords and fought in the first encounter until they were killed in one place.

Abū Mikhnaf related: Zuhayr ibn ʿAbd al-Raḥmān ibn Zuhayr al-Khathʿamī told me: The last one who remained with al-Ḥusayn from his companions was Suwayd ibn ʿAmr ibn Abī al-Muṭāʿ al-Khathʿamī. The first to be killed from Banū Abī Ṭālib that day was ʿAlī al-Akbar ibn al-Ḥusayn ibn ʿAlī, and his mother was Laylā, the daughter of Abī Murrah ibn ʿUrwah ibn Masʿūd al-Thaqafī. He was charging at the people and saying:

> I am ʿAlī
> The son of Ḥusayn
> The son of ʿAlī.
> We, by the Lord of the House,
> are more deserving of the Prophet

By Allah, the son of the illegitimate one
Will not rule over us.

He did that repeatedly. Murrah ibn Munqidh ibn al-Nuʿmān al-ʿAbdī, then al-Laythī, saw him and said: "By the sins of the Arabs, if he passes by me doing what he has been doing, I will make his father bereaved of him." He passed by, charging at the people with his sword. Murrah ibn Munqidh intercepted him, stabbed him, and knocked him down. The people surrounded him and cut him with their swords.

Abū Mikhnaf related: Sulaymān ibn Abī Rāshid told me, from Ḥumayd ibn Muslim al-Azdī, he said: I heard with my own ears that day al-Ḥusayn saying: "May Allah kill the people who killed you, my son! How daring they are against the Most Merciful, and how they violate the sanctity of the Messenger! May the world be ruined after you."

It was as if I saw a woman who resembled like the rising sun, rushing out, calling: "O my brother! O son of my brother!" I asked who she was and it was said: "This is Zaynab, the daughter of Fāṭimah, the daughter of the Messenger of Allah, peace be upon him." She came and threw herself on him. Al-Ḥusayn came and took her by the hand and returned her to the tent.

Al-Ḥusayn approached his son, and his young men came to him, and he said: "Carry your brother." They carried him from the battlefield and placed him in front of the tent where they were fighting.

Then ʿAmr ibn Ṣubayḥ al-Ṣadāʾī shot ʿAbd Allāh ibn Muslim ibn ʿAqīl with an arrow, and he placed his hand on his forehead. He could not move his hands. Then he shot another arrow at him and split his heart. The people attacked them from all sides. ʿAbd Allāh ibn Quṭbah al-Ṭāʾī, then al-Nabhānī, charged at ʿAwn ibn ʿAbd Allāh ibn Jaʿfar ibn Abī Ṭālib and killed him. ʿĀmir ibn Nahshal al-Taymī charged at Muḥammad ibn ʿAbd Allāh ibn Jaʿfar ibn Abī Ṭālib and killed him. ʿUthmān ibn Khālid ibn Asīr al-Juhanī and Bishr ibn Ṣawṭ al-Hamdānī thumma al-Qābiḍī, charged at ʿAbd al-Raḥmān ibn ʿAqīl ibn Abī Ṭālib and killed him. ʿAbd Allāh ibn ʿAzrah al-Khathʿamī shot Jaʿfar ibn ʿAqīl ibn Abī Ṭālib and killed him.

The Killing of the Boy al-Qāsim ibn al-Ḥasan ibn ʿAlī

Abū Mikhnaf related: Sulaymān ibn Abī Rāshid told me, from Ḥumayd ibn Muslim who said: A boy came out to us, his face shining like a piece of the moon, with a sword in his hand, wearing a shirt and a loincloth, and sandals, one of which had a broken strap. I do not forget that it was the left one.

ʿAmr ibn Saʿd ibn Nufayl al-Azdī said to me:"By Allah, I will charge at him." I said to him: "Glory be to Allah! What do you want with that! It is enough for you to kill those you see have surrounded them." He said: "By Allah, I will charge at him."

He charged at him and did not turn back until he struck his head with the sword, and the boy fell on his face. He said: "O uncle!" Al-Ḥusayn rushed like a falcon, then charged like an angry lion, and struck ʿAmr with the sword. ʿAmr defended himself with his arm, and it was cut off from the elbow. He screamed and withdrew. The cavalry of the people of al-Kūfa charged to rescue ʿAmr from al-Ḥusayn. They faced ʿAmr with their chests, moved their hooves, and the horses trampled him until he died.

The dust settled, and I saw al-Ḥusayn standing over the boy, who was kicking his legs. Al-Ḥusayn said:

> Woe to the people who killed you, and who will be their opponent on the Day of Resurrection in your case is your grandfather! By Allah, it is hard for your uncle that you call him and he does not answer you, or he answers you but it does not benefit you! By Allah, many are the voices, and few are the helpers.

Then he carried him, and I saw the boy's legs dragging on the ground. Al-Ḥusayn placed his chest on his chest. I said to myself: "What is he doing with him?" He brought him and laid him with his son ʿAlī ibn al-Ḥusayn and the dead who had been killed around him from his family. I asked about the boy, and it was said: "He is al-Qāsim ibn al-Ḥasan ibn ʿAlī ibn Abī Ṭālib."

Al-Ḥusayn’s Final Fight

Al-Ḥusayn stayed for a long time during the day. Whenever a man from the enemy approached him, he would eventually turn away, out of dislike to kill him and bear the great sin upon himself. A man from Kindah named Mālik ibn al-Nusayr from Banū Badā’ came to him and struck him on the head with the sword. He was wearing a hooded cloak, and the sword cut through the cloak and struck his head, causing his head to bleed. The cloak was filled with blood. Al-Ḥusayn said to him: “May you never eat or drink with it, and may Allah gather you with the wrongdoers!” He threw away the cloak, then called for a cap and wore it, and he was exhausted and less active.

The Kindī man took the cloak - it was made of silk. Later, when he brought it to his wife, Umm ʿAbd Allāh, the daughter of al-Ḥurr, the sister of Ḥusayn ibn al-Ḥurr al-Badī, he began to wash the blood from the cloak. His wife said to him: “You bring the plunder of the son of the daughter of the Messenger of Allah, peace be upon him, into my house! Take it out of here.” His companions mentioned that he remained poor and miserable until he died.

When al-Ḥusayn sat down, a child was brought to him, and he sat him in his lap. They claimed that he was ʿAbd Allāh ibn al-Ḥusayn.

Abū Mikhnaf related: ʿUqbah ibn Bashīr al-Asadī said: Abū Jaʿfar Muḥammad ibn ʿAlī ibn al-Ḥusayn said to me: “We have blood with you, O Banū Asad.” I said: “What is my sin in that, may Allah have mercy on you, O Abā Jaʿfar! And what about it?” He replied: “Al-Ḥusayn was brought a boy, and he was in his lap, when one of you, O Banū Asad, shot him with an arrow and slaughtered him. Al-Ḥusayn caught his blood, and when he filled his hands, he poured it on the ground and said: ‘O Lord, if You have withheld victory from us from the sky, then make that for what is better, and take revenge on these wrongdoers.’”

ʿAbd Allāh ibn ʿUqbah al-Ghanawī shot Abā Bakr ibn al-Ḥusayn ibn ʿAlī with an arrow and killed him. Therefore, the poet, who is Ibn Abī ʿUqbah, said:

> And with Banū Ghanī
> Is a drop of our blood.

And with Banū Asad
Is another
That is counted
And remembered.

It is claimed that al-ʿAbbās ibn ʿAlī said to his brothers from his mother: ʿAbd Allāh, Jaʿfar, and ʿUthmān: "O sons of my mother, advance so that I may inherit you, for you have no children." They did so and were killed.

Hānī ibn Thubayt al-Ḥaḍramī charged at ʿAbd Allāh ibn ʿAlī ibn Abī Ṭālib and killed him. Then he charged at Jaʿfar ibn ʿAlī and killed him and brought his head. Khawli ibn Yazīd al-Aṣbaḥī shot ʿUthmān ibn ʿAlī ibn Abī Ṭālib with an arrow, then a man from Banū Abān ibn Dārm charged at him and killed him and brought his head. A man from Banū Abān ibn Dārm shot Muḥammad ibn ʿAlī ibn Abī Ṭālib and killed him and brought his head.

Hishām said: Abū al-Hudhail, a man from al-Sakūn, told me, from Hānī ibn Thubayt al-Ḥaḍramī who said:

I saw him sitting in the assembly of the Ḥaḍramīs during the time of Khālid ibn ʿAbd Allāh, and he was an old man. I heard him saying:

> I was among those who witnessed the killing of al-Ḥusayn. By Allah, I was standing as the tenth of ten, and there was no man among us except on a horse. The horses were running and neighing, when a boy from the family of al-Ḥusayn came out, holding a stick from those buildings, wearing a loincloth and a shirt, and he was terrified, looking left and right. It was as if I saw two pearls in his ears dangling whenever he turned. A man came running, and when he approached him, he dismounted from his horse, then he went straight to the boy and cut him with the sword.

Hishām said: Al-Sakūnī said: Hānī ibn Thubayt was the one who killed the boy, and when he was blamed for it, he used a pseudonym for himself.

Hishām said: ʿAmr ibn Shimr told me, from Jābir al-Juʿfī who said: Al-Ḥusayn was thirsty such that the thirst became severe for him. He approached to drink water, and Ḥuṣayn ibn Tamīm shot him with an arrow, and it struck his mouth. He began to catch the blood from his mouth and throw it to the sky. Then he praised Allah and extolled Him, then he raised his hands and said: "O Allah, count them in number, and kill them one by one, and do not leave any of them on the earth."

Hishām said, from his father Muḥammad ibn al-Sāʾib, from al-Qāsim ibn al-Aṣbaḥ ibn Nabātah who said: Someone who witnessed al-Ḥusayn in his camp told me that when al-Ḥusayn was overwhelmed in his camp, he rode the causeway intending to reach the Euphrates. A man from Banū Abān ibn Dārm said: "Woe to you! Block him from the water so that his followers do not reach him." He whipped his horse, and the people followed him until they came between him and the Euphrates. Al-Ḥusayn said: "O Allah, make him thirsty," and he shot an arrow, and it struck the palate of al-Ḥusayn. Al-Ḥusayn pulled out the arrow, then spread his hands, and they were filled with blood. Then al-Ḥusayn said: "O Allah, I complain to You about what is being done to the son of the daughter of Your Prophet." He said: By Allah, the man did not stay long until Allah inflicted thirst upon him, and he could not quench his thirst.

Al-Qāsim ibn al-Aṣbaḥ said: I was among those who used to visit that man, and we were cooling him with water, which was cooled with sugar, and there were bowls with milk, and jars with water. He would say: "Woe to you! Give me water, thirst is killing me." He would be given a jar or a bowl that was enough for all the people of the house, and he would drink it. When he took it out of his mouth, he would lie down for a while, then say: "Woe to you! Give me water, thirst is killing me." He said: By Allah, he did not stay long until his stomach burst like the stomach of a camel.

Abū Mikhnaf narrates: Then Shimr ibn Dhī al-Jawshan came with about ten foot soldiers from the people of al-Kūfa towards the place of al-Ḥusayn where his heavy baggage and family were. He walked towards him, and they came between him and his camp. Al-Ḥusayn said: "Woe to you! If you have no religion, and you do not fear the Day of Return, then be free in your worldly affairs, and prevent my camp and my family from your lowly and ignorant ones." Ibn Dhī al-Jawshan said: "That is for you, O son of Fāṭimah and he advanced with the foot soldiers, among whom were Abū al-Junūb - his name was ʿAbd al-Raḥmān al-Juʿfī - and al-Qashʿam ibn ʿAmr ibn Yazīd al-Juʿfī, and Ṣāliḥ ibn Wahb al-Yaznī, and Sinān ibn Anas al-Nakhaʿī, and Khawli ibn Yazīd al-Aṣbaḥī. Shimr ibn Dhī al-Jawshan began to urge them on. He passed by Abū al-Junūb, who was armed, and said to him: "Advance on him!" He replied: "What prevents you from advancing on him yourself?" Shimr said to him: "Do you say that to me!" He said: "And you say that to me!" They began to insult each other. Abū al-Junūb, who was brave, said to him: "By Allah, I almost thrust the spear into your eye." Shimr turned away from him and said: "By Allah, if I can harm you, I will harm you." Then Shimr ibn Dhī al-Jawshan advanced with the foot soldiers towards al-Ḥusayn, and al-Ḥusayn began to charge at them, and they scattered from him.

Then they surrounded him completely, and a boy from his family came to al-Ḥusayn. His sister Zaynab, the daughter of ʿAlī, took him to hold him back. Al-Ḥusayn said to her: "Hold him back." The boy refused and came running to al-Ḥusayn. He stood by his side. He said: Baḥr ibn Kaʿb ibn ʿUbayd Allāh - from Banū Taym Allāh ibn Thaʿlabah ibn ʿUkābah - raised his sword towards al-Ḥusayn. The boy said: "O son of the wicked woman, do you kill my uncle!" He struck him with the sword, and the boy defended himself with his hand, and it was cut off except for the skin, and his hand was hanging. The boy called out: "O mother!" Al-Ḥusayn took him and hugged him to his chest, and said: "O son of my brother, be patient with what has befallen you, and seek the reward in that, for Allah will join you with your righteous ancestors, with the Messenger of Allah, peace be upon him, and ʿAlī ibn Abī Ṭālib, and Ḥamzah, and Jaʿfar, and Ḥasan ibn ʿAlī, peace be upon them all."

Abū Mikhnaf related: Sulaymān ibn Abī Rāshid told me, from Ḥumayd ibn Muslim, he said: I heard al-Ḥusayn that day saying:

> O Allah, withhold from them the rain of the sky, and prevent them from the blessings of the earth. O Allah, if You allow them to enjoy for a while, then divide them into groups, and make them into factions, and never let the rulers be pleased with them, for they invited us to support us, then they attacked us and killed us.

He fought the foot soldiers until they were driven away from him. When al-Ḥusayn was left with three or four men, he called for a pair of trousers with patches that shone brightly, a Yemeni garment, and he tore and knotted it so that it would not be taken from him. One of his companions said to him: "If only you would wear a loincloth underneath it!" He said: "That is a garment of humiliation, and it is not appropriate for me to wear it." When al-Ḥusayn was killed, Baḥr ibn Kaʿb came and stripped him of it, leaving him naked.

Abū Mikhnaf related: ʿAmr ibn Shuʿayb told me, from Muḥammad ibn ʿAbd al-Raḥmān, that the hands of Baḥr ibn Kaʿb would sweat in the winter and dry up in the summer as if they were sticks.

Abū Mikhnaf related: From al-Ḥajjāj, from ʿAbd Allāh ibn ʿAmmār ibn ʿAbd Yaghūth al-Bāriqī who said:

ʿAbd Allāh ibn ʿAmmār was blamed after that for his presence at the killing of al-Ḥusayn. ʿAbd Allāh ibn ʿAmmār said: "I have a favor with Banū Hāshim." We said to him: "What is your favor with them?" He said: "I charged at Ḥusayn with a spear and reached him. By Allah, if I had wanted, I could have stabbed him, but I turned away from him and said: 'What would I gain by killing him! Someone else will kill him.'"

Foot soldiers from his right and left charged at him. He attacked those on his right until they scattered, and those on his left until they scattered. He was wearing a silk shirt and a turban. By Allah, I have never seen a broken man who had lost his son, family, and companions more resolute, more determined, and braver than him. By Allah, I have never seen anyone like him before or after him. The foot soldiers would scatter from his right and left like goats when a wolf attacks them.

By Allah, he was like that when Zaynab, the daughter of Fāṭimah, his sister, came out. It was as if I saw her earring swinging between her ears and shoulders, and she was saying: "I wish the sky would collapse upon the earth!" ʿUmar ibn Saʿd approached Ḥusayn, and she said: "O ʿUmar ibn Saʿd, will Abū ʿAbd Allāh be killed while you watch!" and it was as if I saw ʿUmar's tears flowing down his cheeks and beard. He turned his face away from her.

Abū Mikhnaf related: Ṣaqʿab ibn Zuhayr told me, from Ḥumayd ibn Muslim who said:

Al-Ḥusayn was wearing a silk robe, and he was turbaned, and his hair was dyed with woad. I heard him say before he was killed, while he was fighting on foot like a brave knight, avoiding arrows, and charging at the horses. He said:

> Are you urging each other to kill me! By Allah, you will not kill a servant of Allah after me that Allah will be more angry with you for killing than me. By Allah, I hope that Allah will honor me with your humiliation, and then take revenge on you from where you do not perceive. By Allah, if you kill me, Allah will cast enmity among you and shed your blood, and He will not be pleased with you until He doubles the painful punishment for you.

Al-Ḥusayn stayed for a long time during the day. If the people had wanted to kill him, they could have done so, but they were wary of each other, and each one wanted the others to do the deed.

Shimr called out to the people: "Woe to you, what are you waiting for with this man! Kill him, may your mothers be bereaved of you!" They charged at him from all sides. Zurʿah ibn Sharīk al-Tamīmī struck his left hand, and another struck his shoulder. They withdrew, and he was staggering and falling. He said: Sinān ibn Anas ibn ʿAmr al-Nakhaʿī charged at him and stabbed him with a spear, causing him to fall. Then he said to Khawli ibn Yazīd al-Aṣbaḥī: "Sever his head." He wanted to do it but was too weak and trembled. Sinān ibn Anas said to him: "May Allah break your arms and cut off your hands!" He dismounted, slaughtered him, and severed his head, then gave it to Khawli ibn Yazīd. He had been struck by swords before that.

Abū Mikhnaf related, from Jaʿfar ibn Muḥammad ibn ʿAlī, who said: Al-Ḥusayn was found with thirty-three stab wounds and thirty-four sword strikes when he was killed. Sinān ibn Anas did not let anyone approach al-Ḥusayn except that he charged at them, fearing that they would take his head, until he took al-Ḥusayn's head and gave it to Khawli. Al-Ḥusayn was stripped of what he was wearing. Baḥr ibn Kaʿb took his trousers, Qays ibn al-Ashʿath took his cloak - it was made of silk, and he was called Qays al-Qaṭīfah after that - a man from Banū Awd named al-Aswad took his sandals, and a man from Banū Nahshal ibn Dārm took his sword. It later ended up with the people of Ḥabīb ibn Budayl. The people plundered the saffron, the garments, and the camels. The people attacked the women of al-Ḥusayn, his baggage, and his belongings. The women would struggle to keep their clothes until they were ripped off of them.

Abū Mikhnaf related: Zuhayr ibn ʿAbd al-Raḥmān al-Khathʿamī told me that Suwayd ibn ʿAmr ibn Abī al-Muṭāʿ was struck down and severely wounded. He fell among the dead, severely wounded. He heard them saying: "Al-Ḥusayn has been killed." He regained consciousness, and he had a knife with him and but his sword had been taken. He fought them with his knife for a while, then he was killed. ʿUrwah ibn Buṭṭār al-Taghlibī and Zayd ibn Ruqād al-Janabī killed him. He was the last of Al-Ḥusayn's party to be killed.

Abū Mikhnaf related: Sulaymān ibn Abī Rāshid told me, from Ḥumayd ibn Muslim who said: I reached ʿAlī ibn al-Ḥusayn ibn ʿAlī al-Aṣghar while he was lying on a bed, and he was sick. Shimr ibn Dhī al-Jawshan was with foot soldiers, and they were saying: "Shall we not kill this one?" I said: "Glory be to Allah! Shall we kill the children! This is just a boy." I continued to defend him from everyone who came until ʿUmar ibn Saʿd came and said: "No one should enter the house of these women, and no one should harm this sick boy." Whoever has taken anything from their belongings should return it to them. By Allah, no one returned anything. ʿAlī ibn al-Ḥusayn said: "May Allah reward you well! By Allah, Allah has protected me from harm with your words."

The people said to Sinān ibn Anas: "You killed Ḥusayn ibn ʿAlī, the son of Fāṭimah, the daughter of the Messenger of Allah, peace be upon him. You killed the most important Arab. He came to these people to remove the tyrant over them. Go to your commanders and seek your reward from them. If they gave you the treasures of their houses for killing al-Ḥusayn, it would be little." Sinān rode his horse, and he was a brave poet, and he had a touch of madness. He came and stood at the door of the tent of ʿUmar ibn Saʿd and called out in a loud voice:

> Fill my saddlebags with silver and gold.
> I have killed the veiled king
> I have killed the best of people
> In terms of mother and father
> And the best of them in lineage

ʿUmar ibn Saʿd said: "I testify that you are mad and have never been sane. Bring him to me." When he was brought in, he struck him with a stick and said: "You madman, do you speak these words! By Allah, if Ibn Ziyād heard you, he would strike your neck!"

ʿUmar ibn Saʿd took ʿUqbah ibn Samʿān, who was a servant of al-Rubāb, the daughter of Imruʾ al-Qays al-Kalbīyah, who was the mother of Sukaynah, the daughter of al-Ḥusayn. ʿUmar said to him: "What are you?" He said: "I am a servant," and he let him go. No one else escaped from them except al-Murqaʿ ibn Thumāmah al-Asadī, who had scattered his arrows and knelt on his knees, fighting. A group of his people came to him and said: "You are safe, come out to us." He came out to them. When ʿUmar ibn Saʿd brought them to Ibn Ziyād and informed him of his situation, he sent him to al-Zārah.

ʿUmar ibn Saʿd then called out to his companions: "Who will volunteer to trample al-Ḥusayn with their horse?" Ten men volunteered, including Isḥāq ibn Ḥayywah al-Ḥaḍramī, who took al-Ḥusayn's shirt and later became leprous, and Aḥbash ibn Murthad ibn ʿAlqamah ibn Salāmah al-Ḥaḍramī. They came and trampled al-Ḥusayn with their horses until they crushed his back and chest. I heard that Aḥbash ibn Murthad was later struck by a stray arrow during a battle, and it split his heart, and he died.

Seventy-two men from the companions of al-Ḥusayn were killed. The people of al-Ghāḍiriyyah from Banū Asad buried al-Ḥusayn and his companions a day after they were killed. Eighty-eight men from the companions of ʿUmar ibn Saʿd were killed, not including the wounded. ʿUmar ibn Saʿd prayed over them and buried them.

The Treatment of the Head of al-Ḥusayn

As soon as al-Ḥusayn was killed, his head was sent that same day with Khawli ibn Yazīd and Ḥumayd ibn Muslim al-Azdī to ʿUbayd Allāh ibn Ziyād. Khawli brought it and wanted to enter the palace, but found the door closed. He went to his house and placed it under a washbasin in his house. He had two wives: one from Banū Asad and the other from the Ḥaḍramīs, named al-Nawār, the daughter of Mālik ibn ʿAqrab. That night was the night of the Ḥaḍramī woman.

Hishām related: My father told me, from al-Nawār, the daughter of Mālik, who said:

Khawli brought the head of al-Ḥusayn and placed it under a washbasin in the house. Then he entered the house and went to his bed. I said to him: "What is the news? What do you have?" He said: "I have brought you the wealth of the ages. This is the head of al-Ḥusayn with you in the house."

She said: "I said: Woe to you—people brought gold and silver, and you brought the head of the son of the Messenger of Allah, peace be upon him! By Allah, our heads will never be together in one house." She said: "I got up from my bed and went out to the yard."

He called the Asadī woman and brought her in. I sat watching. She said: "By Allah, I kept watching until I saw a light shining like a column from the sky to the washbasin, and I saw white birds hovering around it."

When morning came, he took the head to ʿUbayd Allāh ibn Ziyād, and ʿUmar ibn Saʿd stayed that day and the next. Then he ordered Ḥumayd ibn Bukayr al-Aḥmarī to announce to the people to depart to al-Kūfa, and he took with him the daughters of al-Ḥusayn, his sisters, and the children who were with him, and ʿAlī ibn al-Ḥusayn was sick.

Let me know if you'd like this adapted for academic formatting or publication.When morning came, he took the head to ʿUbayd Allāh ibn Ziyād, and ʿUmar ibn Saʿd stayed that day and the next. Then he ordered Ḥumayd ibn Bukayr al-Aḥmarī to announce to the people to depart to al-Kūfa, and he took with him the daughters of al-Ḥusayn, his sisters, and the children who were with him, and ʿAlī ibn al-Ḥusayn was sick.

The Treatment of the Women of the Household of the Prophet ﷺ

Abū Mikhnaf related: Abū Zuhayr al-ʿAbsī told me, from Qurrah ibn Qays al-Tamīmī, he said: "I saw those women when they passed by Ḥusayn and his family and children, they screamed and slapped their faces. I intercepted them on a horse, and I have never seen a sight of women more beautiful than the sight I saw of them that day. By Allah, they were more beautiful than the Mahāybirīn."

He said: I have not forgotten the words of Zaynab, the daughter of Fāṭimah, when she passed by her brother al-Ḥusayn lying dead, and she was saying: "O Muḥammad! O Muḥammad! The angels of the sky pray upon you, this is al-Ḥusayn in the open, covered in blood, with his limbs cut off. O Muḥammad! Your daughters are captives, and your descendants are killed, the wind blows upon them." He said: "By Allah, she made every enemy and friend cry."

They gathered the heads of the remaining ones, and sent seventy-two heads with Shimr ibn Dhī al-Jawshan, Qays ibn al-Ash'ath, 'Amr ibn al-Ḥajjāj, and 'Azrah ibn Qays, and they brought them to 'Ubayd Allāh ibn Ziyād.

Abū Mikhnaf related: Sulaymān ibn Abī Rāshid told me, from Ḥumayd ibn Muslim who said:

'Umar ibn Sa'd called me and sent me to his family to give them the good news of Allah's victory and his safety. I went to his family and informed them of that. Then I went until I entered and found Ibn Ziyād sitting with the people, and I found the delegation had arrived. He brought them in and allowed the people to enter. I entered with those who entered, and I saw the head of al-Ḥusayn placed before him, and he was poking at it with a stick between its teeth for a while.

When Zayd ibn Arqam saw him, he said: "Raise this stick from these teeth, for by the One who there is no god but Him, I have seen the lips of the Messenger of Allah, peace be upon him, on these lips, kissing them."

Then the old man burst into tears. Ibn Ziyād said to him: "May Allah make your eyes cry! By Allah, if you were not an old man who has lost his mind, I would have struck your neck."

He said: "He got up and left." When he left, I heard the people saying: "By Allah, Zayd ibn Arqam said something that if Ibn Ziyād had heard, he would have killed him."

I said: "What did he say?" They said: He passed by us saying: "A slave has ruled over a slave, and made them his property. You, O Arabs, are slaves after today. You killed the son of Fāṭimah, and you appointed the son of Marjānah, and he kills your best and enslaves your worst. You have accepted humiliation, so woe to those who accept humiliation!"

Zaynab Bint Fāṭimah's Rebuke of 'Ubayd Allāh ibn Ziyād

When he entered with the head of Ḥusayn, his children, his sisters, and his women to 'Ubayd Allāh ibn Ziyād, Zaynab, the daughter of Fāṭimah, wore her worst clothes and disguised herself, surrounded by her maidservants. When she entered, she sat down. 'Ubayd Allāh ibn Ziyād said: "Who is the woman that is sitting?" She did not speak to him. He said that three times, and each time she did not speak to him. One of her maidservants said: "This is Zaynab, the daughter of Fāṭimah." 'Ubayd Allāh said to her: "Praise be to Allah who exposed you, killed you, and proved your story false!" She said: "Praise be to Allah who honored us with Muḥammad, peace be upon him, and purified us with a thorough purification, not as you say. Only the wicked are exposed, and the liar is proven false." He said: "How did you find Allah's treatment of your family?" She said: "He decreed death for them, and they went out to their resting places, and Allah will gather you and them, and you will argue with Him, and dispute before Him." Ibn Ziyād became angry and furious. 'Amr ibn Ḥurayth said to him: "May Allah rectify the governor! She is only a woman, and is a woman held accountable for her words? She is not held accountable for her speech, nor blamed for her mistakes."

Ibn Ziyād said to her: "Allah has healed my soul from your tyrant and the rebellious sinners of your family." She cried and said: "By my life, you have killed my elder, destroyed my family, cut off my branch, and uprooted my origin. If this heals you, then you have been healed."

'Ubayd Allāh said to her: "This is courage, by my life, your father was a poet and brave." She said: "What does a woman have to do with courage! I have other concerns than courage, but I express what I say."

The Treatment of 'Alī ibn al-Ḥusayn

Abū Mikhnaf, from al-Mujālid ibn Sa'īd, said: When 'Ubayd Allāh ibn Ziyād looked at 'Alī ibn al-Ḥusayn, he said to a guard: "See if he has reached the age of men." He uncovered his garment and said: "Yes." He said: "Take him and strike his neck." 'Alī said to him: "If there is kinship between you and these women, send a man with them to protect them." Ibn Ziyād said to him: "Go!," and he sent 'Alī ibn al-Ḥusayn with them.

Abū Mikhnaf related: As for Sulaymān ibn Abī Rāshid, he told me from Ḥumayd ibn Muslim who said:

I was standing by Ibn Ziyād when ʿAlī ibn al-Ḥusayn was presented to him. He said to him: "What is your name?" He said: "I am ʿAlī ibn al-Ḥusayn." He said: "Did Allah not kill ʿAlī ibn al-Ḥusayn?" He remained silent. Ibn Ziyād said to him: "Why do you not speak?" He said: "I had a brother also named ʿAlī, and the people killed him." He said: "Allah has killed him." He remained silent. Ibn Ziyād said to him: "Why do you not speak?" He said: "Allah takes the souls at the time of their death, and no soul can die except by Allah's permission." He said: "By Allah, you are one of them. Woe to you! See if he has reached maturity. By Allah, I think he is a man." Marī ibn Muʿādh al-Aḥmarī uncovered him and said: "Yes, he has reached maturity." He said: "Kill him."

ʿAlī ibn al-Ḥusayn said: "Who will take care of these women?" Zaynab, his aunt, clung to him and said: "O son of Ziyād, enough of us! Have you not had enough of our blood? Have you left anyone of us?" She embraced him and said: "I ask you by Allah, if you are a believer, if you kill him, then kill me with him!"

ʿAlī called out to him and said: "O son of Ziyād, if there is kinship between you and them, send a pious man with them to accompany them with the companionship of Islam."

He looked at her for a while, then looked at the people and said: "How amazing is kinship! By Allah, I think she wishes that if I killed him, I would kill her with him. Leave the boy, go with your women."

The Boasting of ʿUbayd Allāh ibn Ziyād

Ḥumayd ibn Muslim said: When ʿUbayd Allāh entered the palace and the people entered, it was announced: "The prayer is gathering!" The people gathered in the great mosque. Ibn Ziyād ascended the pulpit and said:

> Praise be to Allah who has manifested the truth and its people, and supported the Commander of the Faithful, Yazīd ibn Muʿāwiyah, and his party, and killed the liar, the son of the liar, al-Ḥusayn ibn ʿAlī, and his followers.

ʿAbd Allāh ibn ʿAfīf al-Azdī, then al-Ghāmidī, then one of Banū Wālibah - who was one of the followers of ʿAlī, may Allah honor his face, and his left eye was lost on the day of the Battle of the Camel with ʿAlī, and on the day of Ṣiffīn he was struck on the head and another on his eyebrow, and his other eye was lost, and he rarely left the great mosque, praying in it until night, then he would leave on hearing the words of Ibn Ziyād, said:

> O son of Marjānah, the liar, the son of the liar, you and your father, and the one who appointed you, and his father. O son of Marjānah, do you kill the sons of the prophets and speak the words of the truthful!

Ibn Ziyād said: "Seize him." The guards jumped on him and took him. He called out with the slogan of al-Azd: "O Mabrūr" - ʿAbd al-Raḥmān ibn Mukhnif al-Azdī was sitting - he said: "Woe to you! You have destroyed yourself and your people." He said: "There were seven hundred fighters from al-Azd present in al-Kūfa that day." Young men from al-Azd jumped on him and took him to his family. He sent someone to bring him, killed him, and ordered him to be crucified in al-Sabkha, and he was crucified there.

Abū Mikhnaf related: ʿUbayd Allāh ibn Ziyād then raised the head of al-Ḥusayn in al-Kūfa and paraded it around al-Kūfa. Then he called Zahr ibn Qays and sent him with the head of al-Ḥusayn and the heads of his companions to Yazīd ibn Muʿāwiyah. Zahr was accompanied by Abū Burdah ibn ʿAwf al-Azdī and Ṭāriq ibn Abī Ẓubayān al-Azdī. They went until they arrived in al-Shām to Yazīd ibn Muʿāwiyah.

The Head of al-Ḥusayn Is Presented to Yazīd ibn Muʿāwiyah

Hishām said: ʿAbd Allāh ibn Yazīd ibn Rūḥ ibn Zunbāʿ al-Judhāmī told me, from his father, from al-Ghāz ibn Rabīʿah al-Jurashī, from Ḥimyar, he said: "By Allah, we were with Yazīd ibn Muʿāwiyah in Damascus when Zahr ibn Qays came and entered upon Yazīd ibn Muʿāwiyah."

Yazīd said to him: "Woe to you! What is behind you? What do you have?"

He said:

> Rejoice, O Commander of the Faithful, with Allah's victory and support. Al-Ḥusayn ibn ʿAlī came to us with eighteen of his family and sixty of his followers. We marched to them, asked them to surrender and submit to the judgment of the governor, ʿUbayd Allāh ibn Ziyād, or fight. They chose to fight over surrender.
>
> We attacked them at sunrise, surrounded them from all sides, and when the swords took their toll on the heads of the people, they fled without refuge, seeking shelter from us in the hills and pits, as pigeons seek shelter from a hawk.
>
> By Allah, O Commander of the Faithful, it was only like the slaughter of a camel or the nap of a sleeper until we came upon the last of them. There are their bodies stripped, their clothes torn, their cheeks covered in dust, the sun scorching them, and the wind blowing upon them, their visitors are eagles and vultures in the desert."

Yazīd's eyes filled with tears, and he said: "I would have been satisfied with your obedience without killing al-Ḥusayn. May Allah curse the son of Sumayyah! By Allah, if I had been his companion, I would have forgiven him. May Allah have mercy on al-Ḥusayn!"

He did not reward him with anything.

He said: ʿUbayd Allāh then ordered the women and children of al-Ḥusayn to be prepared, and ordered ʿAlī ibn al-Ḥusayn to be shackled with a collar around his neck. Then he sent them with Maḥfiz ibn Thaʿlabah al-ʿĀʾidhī, ʿĀʾidhah Quraysh, and Shimr ibn Dhī al-Jawshan. They went with them until they arrived at Yazīd. ʿAlī ibn al-Ḥusayn did not speak a word to either of them on the way until they arrived. When they reached the door of Yazīd, Maḥfiz ibn Thaʿlabah raised his voice and said: "This is Maḥfiz ibn Thaʿlabah who has brought the wicked and immoral to the Commander of the Faithful." Yazīd ibn Muʿāwiyah replied: "What a wicked and immoral mother gave birth to Maḥfiz."

Abū Mikhnaf related: Ṣaqʿab ibn Zuhayr told me, from al-Qāsim ibn ʿAbd al-Raḥmān, the servant of Yazīd ibn Muʿāwiyah, he said: When the heads were placed before Yazīd - the head of al-Ḥusayn and his family and companions - Yazīd said:

> They split open the skulls of men of honor
> upon us,
> though they were more disobedient and more unjust.
> Indeed, by Allah, O Ḥusayn, if it had been your companion (ruler),
> we would not have killed you.

Abū Mikhnaf related: Abū Jaʿfar al-ʿAbsī told me, from Abū ʿAmārah al-ʿAbsī, who said:

Yaḥyā ibn al-Ḥakam, the brother of Marwān ibn al-Ḥakam, said:

> A piece of meat beside Ṭaff (i.e., the site of Karbala) has closer
> kinship...
> than Ibn Ziyād, the slave with corrupted lineage.
> Sumayyah's offspring have become as numerous as pebbles...
> while the daughter of the Messenger of Allah has no offspring.'"

He said: Yazīd ibn Muʿāwiyah struck Yaḥyā ibn al-Ḥakam on the chest and said: "Be quiet."

When Yazīd ibn Muʿāwiyah sat, he called the nobles of al-Shām and seated them around him. Then he called for ʿAlī ibn al-Ḥusayn, the children of al-Ḥusayn, and his women, and they were brought before him while the people were watching. Yazīd said to ʿAlī: "O ʿAlī, your father is the one who severed my kinship, ignored my right, and disputed my authority. Allah has done to him what you have seen!" ʿAlī said:

"*No disaster strikes on the earth or in yourselves except that it is in a Book before We bring it into being.*" (Sūrat al-Ḥadīd, 57:22).

Yazīd said to his son Khālid: Respond to him. Khālid did not know what to say, so Yazīd said to him: Say:

And whatever affliction befalls you is because of what your own hands have earned and He pardons much. (Surah ash-Shūra, 42:30)

After that exchange he left him alone.

Yazīd ibn Muʿāwiyah's Treatment of the Captive Womenfolk of al-Ḥusayn

Then he called for the women and children and seated them before him. He saw their poor condition and said: "May Allah curse Ibn Marjānah! If there had been any kinship or relationship between him and you, he would not have done this to you, nor sent you like this."

Abū Mikhnaf related, from al-Ḥārith ibn Kaʿb, from Fāṭimah bint ʿAlī who said: When we were seated before Yazīd ibn Muʿāwiyah, he showed us compassion, ordered something for us, and treated us kindly. Then a red-faced man from al-Shām stood up and said to Yazīd: "O Commander of the Faithful, give me this one" - meaning me, and I was a beautiful girl. I trembled and was frightened, thinking that it was permissible for them. I took hold of my sister Zaynab's clothes. She said: "My sister Zaynab was older and wiser than me, and she knew that it was not permissible." She said: "You have lied, by Allah, and you have been disgraceful! That is not for you or him."

Yazīd became angry and said: "You have lied, by Allah, that is for me, and if I wanted to do it, I would have done it." She said: "No, by Allah, Allah has not made that permissible for you unless you leave our religion and follow a different religion." Yazīd became even angrier and said: "Do you address me like this! It was your father and your brother who left the religion." Zaynab said: "By the religion of Allah, the religion of my father, the religion of my brother, and the religion of my grandfather, you and your father and your grandfather were guided." He said: "You have lied, O enemy of Allah." She said: "You are a tyrant ruler, you insult unjustly, and you oppress with your authority." By Allah, it was as if he was ashamed and fell silent.

Then the man from al-Shām returned and said: "O Commander of the Faithful, give me this girl." Yazīd said: "Go away, may Allah grant you a decisive death!" Then Yazīd ibn Muʿāwiyah said: "O Nuʿmān ibn Bashīr, prepare them with what they need, and send with them a trustworthy and righteous man from the people of al-Shām, and send with him horses and helpers to take them to al-Madīnah."

Then he ordered the women to be housed in a separate house, with what they needed, and their brother ʿAlī ibn al-Ḥusayn with them in the house they were in. They left until they entered the house of Yazīd, and no woman from the family of Muʿāwiyah remained except that she met them, crying and mourning for al-Ḥusayn. They mourned for him for three days. Yazīd did not have lunch or dinner except that he invited ʿAlī ibn al-Ḥusayn to join him. He invited him one day, and he invited ʿUmar ibn al-Ḥasan ibn ʿAlī, who was a young boy. He said to ʿUmar ibn al-Ḥasan: "Will you fight this boy?" meaning his son Khālid. He said: "No, but give me a knife and give him a knife, then I will fight him." Yazīd took him and hugged him, then said: "A snake gives birth to nothing but a snake!"

When they wanted to leave, Yazīd called ʿAlī ibn al-Ḥusayn and said: "May Allah curse Ibn Marjānah. By Allah, if I had been his companion, he would not have asked me for anything except that I would have given it to him, and I would have protected him from death with everything I could, even if it meant the destruction of some of my children. But Allah has decreed what you have seen. Write to me and let me know of any need you have."

He clothed them and entrusted them to that messenger. They left, and he traveled with them at night, keeping them in front of him so that they would not escape his sight. When they stopped, he would move away from them, and he and his companions would spread out around them like guards. He would stay close enough that if any of them needed to perform ablution or relieve themselves, they would not feel embarrassed. He continued to accompany them on the road like this, asking about their needs and treating them kindly until they entered al-Madīnah.

Al-Ḥārith ibn Kaʿb said: Fāṭimah bint ʿAlī said to me:

> I said to my sister Zaynab: "O sister, this Shāmī man has been kind to us during our journey, shall we reward him?" She said: "By Allah, we have nothing to reward him with except our jewelry." I said to her: "Then let us give him our jewelry." I took my bracelets and anklets, and my sister took her bracelet and anklet, and we sent them to him, apologizing and saying: "This is your reward for your kindness to us." He said:" If what you did was for the world, your jewelry would have satisfied me and more, but by Allah, I did it

only for Allah and for your kinship with the Messenger of Allah, peace be upon him."

Hishām said: As for ʿAwānah ibn al-Ḥakam al-Kalbī, he said: When al-Ḥusayn was killed and the captives and the spoils were brought to ʿUbayd Allāh in al-Kūfah while the people were detained, a stone fell into the prison with a letter tied to it. The letter read:

> The courier left with your order on such and such a day to Yazīd ibn Muʿāwiyah, and he will travel for such and such days and return in such and such days. If you hear the *takbīr*, be certain of death, and if you do not hear the *takbīr*, it is safety, if Allah wills.

Two or three days before the courier's arrival, another stone was thrown into the prison with a letter and a knife. The letter said:

> Make your wills and prepare, for the courier is expected on such and such a day.

The courier arrived, and they did not hear the takbīr, and a letter came ordering the release of the captives.

ʿUbayd Allāh called Maḥfiz ibn Thaʿlabah and Shimr ibn Dhī al-Jawshan and said: Take the captives and the head to the Commander of the Faithful, Yazīd ibn Muʿāwiyah. They left and arrived at Yazīd. Maḥfiz ibn Thaʿlabah stood up and shouted: "We have brought the head of the most foolish and wicked of people." Yazīd said: "The mother of Maḥfiz did not give birth to a more foolish and wicked person, rather he is a severer of ties and a wrongdoer." When Yazīd saw the head of al-Ḥusayn, he said:

> They split the heads of noble men
> Against us, and they were the most disobedient and oppressive.

Then he said: "Do you know why this happened? He used to say, "My father ʿAlī is better than his father, my mother Fāṭimah is better than his mother, my grandfather the Messenger of Allah is better than his grandfather, and I am better than him and more deserving of this matter than him." As for his saying: "His father is better than my father," my father disputed with his father, and the people knew which of them was judged in his favor. As for his saying: "My mother is better than his mother," by my life, Fāṭimah, the daughter of the Messenger of Allah, peace be upon him, is better than my mother. As for his saying: "My grandfather is better than his grandfather," by my life, no one who believes in Allah and the Last Day sees anyone equal to the Messenger of Allah or a rival to him. But he was only deceived by his understanding, and he did not read: *Say, O Allah, Owner of Sovereignty, You give sovereignty to whom You will and take sovereignty away from whom You will. You honor whom You will and humble whom You will. In Your hand is [all] good. Indeed, You are over all things competent.* (Surah Āli-ʿImrān 3:26)

Then the women of al-Ḥusayn were brought to Yazīd, and the women of Yazīd's family and the daughters of Muʿāwiyah and his family cried and wailed. Then they were brought to Yazīd, and Fāṭimah bint al-Ḥusayn, who was older than Sukaynah, said: "Are the daughters of the Messenger of Allah captives, O Yazīd!" Yazīd said: "O daughter of my brother, I did not want this." She said: "By Allah, nothing is left for us." He said: "O daughter of my brother, what I have given you is greater than what was taken from you." Then they were taken out and brought to the house of Yazīd ibn Muʿāwiyah. No woman from the family of Yazīd remained except that she came to them, and they held mourning for three days. Yazīd sent to each woman: "What was taken from you?" There was no woman who claimed anything, no matter how much, except that he doubled it for her. Sukaynah used to say: "I have not seen a man who disbelieves in Allah better than Yazīd ibn Muʿāwiyah."

Then the captives were brought to him, including ʿAlī ibn al-Ḥusayn. Yazīd said to him: "Oh, ʿAlī!" ʿAlī said: "*No disaster strikes upon the earth or among yourselves except that it is in a register before We bring it into being - indeed that, for Allah, is easy. So that you do not grieve over what has passed you, nor rejoice over what has come to you, and Allah does not love every boastful and proud person.* (Sūrat al-Ḥadīd 57:22-23)

Yazīd replied: *And whatever misfortune befalls you, it is because of what your hands have earned, and He pardons much.* (Surah ash-Shūrā 42:30) Then he prepared him, gave him money, and sent him to al-Madīnah.

Hishām said, from Abū Mikhnaf: Abū Ḥamzah al-Thumālī told me, from ʿAbd Allāh al-Thumālī, from al-Qāsim ibn Bukhayt who said: When the delegation from al-Kūfah arrived with the head of al-Ḥusayn, they entered the mosque of Damascus. Marwān ibn al-Ḥakam said to them: "How did you do?" They said: "Eighteen men came to us, and by Allah, we wiped them out to the last one. These are the heads and captives." Marwān jumped up and left.

Marwān's brother Yaḥyā ibn al-Ḥakam came to them and said: "What did you do?" They repeated their words to him. He said: "You have blocked yourselves from Muḥammad on the Day of Resurrection. I will never join you in any matter." Then he got up and left.

They entered upon Yazīd and placed the head before him, and told him the story. Hind bint ʿAbd Allāh ibn ʿĀmir ibn Kurayz - who was the wife of Yazīd ibn Muʿāwiyah - heard the conversation. She covered herself with her garment and went out, saying: "O Commander of the Faithful, is this the head of al-Ḥusayn ibn Fāṭimah, the daughter of the Messenger of Allah!" He said: "Yes, so mourn for him, and lament for the son of the daughter of the Messenger of Allah, peace be upon him, and the pure one of Quraysh. Ibn Ziyād hastened to kill him, may Allah kill him!" Then he allowed the people to enter, and the head was before him. Yazīd had a stick and was poking at the mouth of the head. Then he said:

This is as al-Ḥuṣayn ibn al-Ḥammām al-Murrī said:

> They split the heads of noble men
> Against us, and they were the most disobedient and oppressive.

A man from the Companions of the Messenger of Allah, peace be upon him, named Abū Barzah al-Aslamī said: "Do you poke at the mouth of al-Ḥusayn with your stick! By Allah, your stick has taken its place in his mouth. I have seen the Messenger of Allah, peace be upon him, kissing it. By Allah, Yazīd, you will come on the Day of Resurrection with Ibn Ziyād as your intercessor, and this one will come on the Day of Resurrection with Muḥammad, peace be upon him, as his intercessor." Then he got up and left.

Announcement of the Martyrdom of al-Ḥusayn at al-Madīnah

Hishām said: ʿAwānah ibn al-Ḥakam told me, he said: When ʿUbayd Allāh ibn Ziyād killed al-Ḥusayn ibn ʿAlī and brought his head to him, he called ʿAbd al-Malik ibn Abī al-Ḥārith al-Sulamī and said: "Go to al-Madīnah and inform ʿAmr ibn Saʿīd ibn al-ʿĀṣ of the killing of al-Ḥusayn" - and ʿAmr ibn Saʿīd ibn al-ʿĀṣ was the governor of al-Madīnah at that time. He said: "Go and do not let the news precede you." He gave him dinars and said: "Do not make excuses for lagging behind and if your mount fails you, buy another mount." ʿAbd al-Malik said: "I arrived in al-Madīnah, and a man from Quraysh met me and said: 'What is the news?' I said: 'The news is with the governor.' He said: '*Indeed, we belong to Allah, and indeed to Him we will return*! al-Ḥusayn ibn ʿAlī has been killed.' I entered upon ʿAmr ibn Saʿīd and he said: "What is behind you?" I said: "What is the secret of the governor?" al-Ḥusayn ibn ʿAlī has been killed. He said: "Announce his killing." So I announced his killing. By Allah, I have never heard a wailing like the wailing of the women of Banū Hāshim in their homes for al-Ḥusayn. ʿAmr ibn Saʿīd laughed and said:

> The women of Banū Ziyād wailed
> like the wailing of our women on the day of al-Arnab.

Al-Arnab was a battle that took place between Banū Zubayd and Banū Ziyād from Banū al-Ḥārith ibn Kaʿb, from the clan of ʿAbd al-Madān. This verse is by ʿAmr ibn Maʿdīkarib. Then ʿAmr said: "This wailing is like the wailing for ʿUthmān ibn ʿAffān." Then he ascended the pulpit and informed the people of his killing.

Hishām said, from Abū Mikhnaf, from Sulaymān ibn Abī Rāshid, from ʿAbd al-Raḥmān ibn ʿUbayd Abī al-Kunūd, he said: When ʿAbd Allāh ibn Jaʿfar ibn Abī Ṭālib heard of the killing of his two sons with al-Ḥusayn, some of his servants entered upon him, and the people were consoling him. He said: "I do not think that servant was anyone but Abū al-Laslās." He said: "This is what we have received and what has come upon us from al-Ḥusayn!" ʿAbd Allāh ibn Jaʿfar threw his sandal at him and said: "O son of a harlot, do you say this about al-Ḥusayn! By Allah, if I had been present, I would have loved not to leave him until I was killed with him. By Allah, what makes me content with their loss and eases my grief over them is that they were struck down with my brother and cousin, supporting him and being patient with him." Then he turned to his companions and said: "Praise be to Allah, the Mighty and Majestic, for the martyrdom of al-Ḥusayn. If my hand did not support al-Ḥusayn, my sons did."

When the people of al-Madīnah heard of the killing of al-Ḥusayn, the daughter of ʿAqīl ibn Abī Ṭālib came out with her women, uncovered, twisting her garment, and saying:

> What will you say when the Prophet asks you.
> What did you do while you were the last of the nations
> With my family and my people after my passing
> Some of them captives and some of them covered in blood!

Hishām said, from ʿAwānah, he said: ʿUbayd Allāh ibn Ziyād said to ʿUmar ibn Saʿd after killing al-Ḥusayn: "O ʿUmar, where is the letter I wrote to you about killing al-Ḥusayn?" He said: "I carried out your order, and the letter was lost." He said: "You will bring it to me." He said: "It was lost." He said: "By Allah, you will bring it to me!" He said: "By Allah, it was read to the old women of Quraysh as an apology to them in al-Madīnah. By Allah, I advised you about al-Ḥusayn with advice that if I had given it to Saʿd ibn Abī Waqqāṣ, I would have fulfilled his right." ʿUthmān ibn Ziyād, the brother of ʿUbayd Allāh, said: "By Allah, it is true. I wish that there was not a man from Banū Ziyād except that there was a ring in his nose until the Day of Resurrection and that al-Ḥusayn was not killed. By Allah, ʿUbayd Allāh did not deny that."

Hishām said: Some of our companions told me, from ʿAmr ibn Abī al-Muqaddām, he said: ʿAmr ibn ʿIkrimah told me: We woke up on the morning of the killing of al-Ḥusayn in al-Madīnah, and a servant of ours was telling us, he said: I heard a caller last night calling out and saying:

> O ignorant killers of al-Ḥusayn
> Rejoice in punishment and torment
> All the inhabitants of the sky pray against you
> From prophets, angels, and tribes
> You have been cursed by the tongue of David
> And Moses and the bearer of the Gospel

Hishām said: ʿUmar ibn Ḥayzūm al-Kalbī told me, from his father who said: "I heard that voice."

Names of the Companions of al-Ḥusayn Who Were Killed

Mention of the names of those who were killed from Banū Hāshim with al-Ḥusayn and the number of those killed from each tribe that fought him. Hishām said: Abū Mikhnaf related: When al-Ḥusayn ibn ʿAlī was killed, the heads of those who were killed with him from his family, followers, and supporters were brought to ʿUbayd Allāh ibn Ziyād. Kinda brought thirteen heads, and their leader was Qays ibn al-Ashʿath. Hawāzin brought twenty heads, and their leader was Shimr ibn Dhī al-Jawshan. Tamīm brought seventeen heads. Banū Asad brought six heads. Madhḥij brought seven heads. The rest of the army brought seven heads, totaling seventy heads.

1. Al-Ḥusayn ibn ʿAlī (mother: Fāṭimah, daughter of the Messenger of Allah ﷺ)
   → Killed by: Sinān ibn Anas al-Nakhaʿī, then al-Aṣbaḥī
   → Head brought by: Khawli ibn Yazīd
2. Al-ʿAbbās ibn ʿAlī ibn Abī Ṭālib (mother: Umm al-Banīn)
   → Killed by: Zayd ibn Ruqād al-Janabī and Ḥakīm ibn al-Ṭufayl al-Sanbasī
3. Jaʿfar ibn ʿAlī ibn Abī Ṭālib (mother: Umm al-Banīn)
4. ʿAbd Allāh ibn ʿAlī ibn Abī Ṭālib (mother: Umm al-Banīn)
5. ʿUthmān ibn ʿAlī ibn Abī Ṭālib (mother: Umm al-Banīn)
   → Killed by: Khawli ibn Yazīd (arrow)
6. Muḥammad ibn ʿAlī ibn Abī Ṭālib (mother: a slave woman)
   → Killed by: A man from Banū Abān ibn Dārm
7. Abū Bakr ibn ʿAlī ibn Abī Ṭālib (mother: Laylā bint Masʿūd al-Dārmīyah)
   → Killed (with some doubt)
8. ʿAlī ibn al-Ḥusayn ibn ʿAlī (mother: Laylā bint Abī Murrah al-Thaqafīyah)
   → Killed by: Murrah ibn Munqidh al-ʿAbdī
9. ʿAbd Allāh ibn al-Ḥusayn ibn ʿAlī (mother: al-Rubāb bint Imruʾ al-Qays)
   → Killed by: Hānī ibn Thubayt al-Ḥaḍramī
10. ʿAlī ibn al-Ḥusayn ibn ʿAlī (a different son; too young)
    → Survived
11. Abū Bakr ibn al-Ḥasan ibn ʿAlī (mother: a slave woman)
    → Killed by: ʿAbd Allāh ibn ʿUqbah al-Ghanawī
12. ʿAbd Allāh ibn al-Ḥasan ibn ʿAlī (mother: a slave woman)
    → Killed by: Ḥarmalah ibn Kāhin (arrow)

13. Al-Qāsim ibn al-Ḥasan ibn ʿAlī (mother: a slave woman)
    → Killed by: Saʿd ibn ʿAmr ibn Nufayl al-Azdī
14. ʿAwn ibn ʿAbd Allāh ibn Jaʿfar (mother: Jumānah bint al-Musayyib al-Fazārīyah)
    → Killed by: ʿAbd Allāh ibn Quṭbah al-Ṭāʾī, then al-Nabhānī
15. Muḥammad ibn ʿAbd Allāh ibn Jaʿfar (mother: al-Khawṣāʾ bint Khuṣafah al-Bakrīyah)
    → Killed by: ʿĀmir ibn Nahshal al-Taymī
16. Jaʿfar ibn ʿAqīl ibn Abī Ṭālib (mother: Umm al-Banīn bint al-Shaqr)
    → Killed by: Bishr ibn Ḥawṭ al-Hamdānī
17. ʿAbd al-Raḥmān ibn ʿAqīl (mother: a slave woman)
    → Killed by: ʿUthmān ibn Khālid ibn Asīr al-Juhanī
18. ʿAbd Allāh ibn ʿAqīl ibn Abī Ṭālib (mother: a slave woman)
    → Killed by: ʿAmr ibn Ṣubayḥ al-Ṣadāʾī
19. Muslim ibn ʿAqīl ibn Abī Ṭālib (mother: a slave woman)
    → Killed (born in al-Kūfa)
20. ʿAbd Allāh ibn Muslim ibn ʿAqīl (mother: Ruqayyah bint ʿAlī ibn Abī Ṭālib)
    → Killed by: ʿAmr ibn Ṣubayḥ al-Ṣadāʾī or Usayd ibn Mālik al-Ḥaḍramī (variant report)
21. Muḥammad ibn Abī Saʿīd ibn ʿAqīl (mother: a slave woman)
    → Killed by: Laqīṭ ibn Yāsir al-Juhanī
22. Al-Ḥasan ibn al-Ḥasan ibn ʿAlī (mother: Khawlah bint Manẓūr al-Fazārīyah)
    → Too young; not killed
23. ʿUmar ibn al-Ḥasan ibn ʿAlī (mother: a slave woman)
    → Too young; not killed
24. Sulaymān (servant of al-Ḥusayn)
    → Killed by: Sulaymān ibn ʿAwf al-Ḥaḍramī
25. Munjiḥ (servant of al-Ḥusayn)
26. ʿAbd Allāh ibn Buqṭar (foster brother of al-Ḥusayn)

Abū Mikhnaf related: ʿAbd al-Raḥmān ibn Jundub al-Azdī told me that after the killing of al-Ḥusayn, ʿUbayd Allāh ibn Ziyād inspected the nobles of al-Kūfa and did not see ʿUbayd Allāh ibn al-Ḥurr. Then he came to him after a few days and entered upon him. He said: "Where were you, O son of al-Ḥurr?" He said: "I was sick." He said: "Sick in heart or sick in body?" He said: "As for my heart, it was not sick, and as for my body, Allah has granted me health." Ibn Ziyād said to him: "You lie, but you were with our enemy." He said: "If I were with your enemy, my place would have been seen, and someone like me would not be hidden."

Ibn Ziyād was distracted for a moment, and Ibn al-Ḥurr left and mounted his horse. Ibn Ziyād said: Where is Ibn al-Ḥurr? They said: "He just left." He said: "Bring him to me." The guards were brought, and they said to him: "Answer the governor." He spurred his horse and said: "Tell him that I will never come to him willingly, by Allah." Then he left and went to the house of Aḥmar ibn Ziyād al-Ṭāʾī, where his companions gathered around him. Then he went to Karbalāʾ and looked at the places where the people had fallen, seeking forgiveness for them, he and his companions. Then he continued until he settled in al-Madāʾin and said:

> The treacherous governor says:
> Oh, if only I had fought for the martyr,
> the son of Fāṭimah!
> Oh, my regret for not having supported him
> Oh, every soul that does not support is regretful
> And because I was not among his protectors
> I have a sorrow that never leaves me
> May Allah water the souls of those
> who girded themselves
> For his victory with a continuous rain
> I stood by their graves and their places
> My heart almost burst
> and my eyes were filled with tears
> By my life, they were valiant in battle
> Swift to the fray, protectors with sharp swords
> They supported the victory of the son
> of their Prophet's daughter
> With their swords, lions of the forest,
> fierce and strong
> If they are killed, every pious soul
> On earth has become sorrowful for that
> And those who see have not seen better than them
> In death, leaders and shining stars
> Do you kill them unjustly
> and hope for our friendship

Abandon a plan that is not suitable for us!
By my life, you have angered us by killing them
How many of us are angry with you and resentful
I have often thought of leading an army
To a group that has strayed from the truth, oppressors
So desist, or I will drive you in battalions
More severe upon you
than the armies of the Daylamites

www.ingramcontent.com/pod-product-compliance
Lightning Source LLC
Chambersburg PA
CBHW030522080526
44586CB00011B/293